MEN-AT-ARMS S
EDITOR: MARTIN W

The Boxer Rebellion

Text by LYNN E. BODIN

Colour plates by CHRIS WARNER

OSPREY PUBLISHING LONDON

Published in 1979 by
Osprey Publishing Ltd
Member company of the George Philip Group
12−14 Long Acre, London WC2E 9LP
© Copyright 1979 Osprey Publishing Ltd
Reprinted 1982, 1983, 1985 (twice), 1987 (twice)

ISBN 0 85045 335 6

Filmset in Great Britain
Printed in Hong Kong

Acknowledgements
The author would like to thank the following,
without whose help this book would not have been
possible: The National Army Museum, London;
The University of Washington Library System,
Seattle (especially Mr Ju Yen Teng in the East Asia
Library) Instructional Media Services, Production
Services Branch, University of Washington, Seattle;
Mr Otto von Sydow for his help in translating
German source material; Mr L. Donald Bartholomew
and Ms Gaie G. Richardson for their critical
comments; and The University of Western Australia
Press, Perth, for allowing the author to use material
from the book *The Siege of the Peking Legations:
A Diary*, L. R. Marchant (ed.).
  Portions of the text of this book originally appeared
in *Savage and Soldier* magazine, Vol. IX No. 2,
May–June 1977.

Introduction

In the year 1900, an unprecedented alliance occurred between the eight major military powers of the world. Never before, and never since, has there been such an alliance. For more than a year military and naval personnel from Austria-Hungary, France, Germany, Great Britain, Italy, Japan, Russia and the United States fought together against a common enemy. That common enemy was a society whose goal was the extermination of all 'foreign devils' in China—the Boxers.

The exact origin of the *I Ho Ch'uan* (Righteous Harmonious Fists), or Boxers as they were called by Westerners, may never be known. Like most Chinese secret societies their past is shrouded in myth and legend. They must have existed in the 1700s, for some Jesuits were expelled from China in 1747 as a result of Boxer influence. Why they were able to rise to such power in 1900 may also remain a mystery. There were certainly Boxers and Boxer sympathizers in positions of influence in the Imperial Court of the Dowager Empress, Tzu Hsi—most notably Prince Tuan.

Though not a Boxer, Tzu Hsi was sympathetic towards the Boxer movement. Her own rise to power began in 1850 when she became a concubine to the Emperor Hsien-Feng. She soon became his favourite and bore him a son who was named as his successor. Tzu Hsi gained the support of the palace eunuchs and the Imperial Guard. In 1861, Hsien-Feng died and Tzu Hsi became regent until her son, Tung Chih, came of age in 1872. Tung Chih was in poor health and lived for only three years after assuming the throne. Tzu Hsi again assumed the regency, this time for her nephew, Kuang Hsü, until 1889. When Kuang Hsü ascended to the throne the real power remained with the Dowager Empress. The Emperor was kept in seclusion and was not allowed to meet with foreign diplomats. To Tzu Hsi, the foreign emissaries in China were troublemakers and in the Boxer movement she saw the possibility of eliminating them without Imperial intervention.

This 'unofficial' Imperial support was not the only factor in the rise of the Boxers. Natural disasters as well as political, economic and military sanctions imposed by the Western Powers and Japan aided in the emergence of the movement.

An artist's impression of a 'Boxer'. (Illustrated London News)

Two successive harvests had failed. The crop failures caused widespread famine, and a plague of locusts only added to the suffering. As if this was not enough, the Yellow River had overflowed its banks and flooded hundreds of villages.

The Chinese people could do little about the natural disasters, but they felt that they could do something about the foreigners and their modern ideas. China's defeat by Japan in the 1894-95 War was the harbinger of encroachments by other 'modern' powers during the last decade of the 19th century. The Germans, in 1896, seized Kiaochow and Tsingtao after two German priests were murdered. The Russians demanded and obtained a lease on Port Arthur and Darien. The French seized Kwangchowwan in the south, and the British obtained a twenty-five-year lease on Wei-Hai-Wei. Finally, the completion of the Tientsin-to-Peking railroad put thousands of Chinese boatmen and cart drivers out of business. Natural disasters had weakened the Chinese people and Western technology had lowered them to the point where they feared becoming merely servants to the intruding foreigners.

People started turning to secret societies which preached hatred of foreigners—and especially to the Boxers. For centuries the Boxers had been preaching against Manchu power as well as against foreign influence. During 1898 and 1899 they emerged from their clandestine meeting rooms and began emphasizing their chauvinism. The Boxers preached extermination or expulsion of 'foreign devils' through ritual use of the martial arts and traditional Chinese weapons. They preached that 'true believers' would be immune to Western weapons. To the Boxers, their enemies were 'devils': all foreigners were 'first-class devils', Chinese Christian converts were 'second-class devils', and those who worked for foreigners were 'third-class devils'.

Superstitions and magical rituals accompanied the Boxer movement. Incantations were used to induce trance-like states among their followers. Some recruiting demonstrations included a shaman shooting a musket (loaded with a blank charge) at a 'faithful' follower, who was not affected. Claims of invulnerability and the promised protection of China's ancient gods were the prime attractions of the Boxer movement. The

An obviously posed photo of a 'Boxer standard bearer'—note spear, and wicker shield; and the Chinese characters fo I Ho Ch'uan—'Righteous Harmonious Fists', or Boxers (Photo: National Army Museum, London)

Boxers employed strong propaganda through a network of printing presses; tens of thousands o leaflets and handbills were distributed, accusing the Catholic Church of committing atrocities or Chinese women and children. Other proclamations promised the return of the rains and o bountiful harvests.

Initially, the Chinese Government attempted to suppress the Boxer movement, but eventually the expeditions against them were halted. Military commanders and provincial governors who were aggressively anti-Boxer were relieved of thei commands or removed from office. During mos of 1899 the Boxers vented their anger on Chines

4

Christians. Many homes and businesses were destroyed, but few people were actually killed.

On 30 December 1899 the first white Christian was killed by the Boxers—a British missionary, the Reverend S. M. Brooks. A series of strong protests by the British and Germans followed almost immediately. As a result of the protests, two Boxers were executed and a third was sentenced to life imprisonment. The Governor of Shantung Province (where the murder took place) was replaced by an ex-military man, Yüan Shih-K'ai. Yüan was a firm law-and-order man, who was a welcome appointment for the foreigners.

On 11 January 1900 the Dowager Empress released an Imperial Edict. Tzu Hsi stated in her decree that China's secret societies were a part of Chinese life and should not be confused with the criminal element. She declared that peaceful citizens who banded together and practised the martial arts for their self-defence should not be branded as hostile to Christians and whites by the foreigners. The foreign diplomats in Peking were outraged, and protested to the Empress about the wording of the decree. Their protests fell on deaf ears. To make matters worse, three edicts were issued warning Governor Yüan Shih-K'ai about using only military force against the Boxers. Tzu Hsi had done everything she could short of openly supporting the Boxer movement.

By the spring of 1900 the Boxer movement was out of control. Seventy Chinese Christians were massacred at Pao Ting Fu, about sixty miles south-west of Peking. On 28 May another riot at Pao Ting Fu, which coincided with several others along the incomplete railway line to Peking, resulted in the destruction of foreign property and the loss of many foreign lives. On the next day, two British missionaries were attacked; one was killed immediately and the other was put to death on the 30th. The foreign diplomats in Peking protested; they gave the Chinese government just twenty-four hours to put down the Boxers, or they themselves would call up troops from the coast.

Before the ministers received their reply, they heard of more riots and destruction between Peking and Pao Ting Fu. The telegraph line to Pao Ting Fu had been cut. The railway station, shops, locomotives and passenger cars at Feng Tai junction were burned. The troops were ordered up from the coast, but their advance was halted by the Chinese. Finally, early on 31 May, permission was granted for the troops to advance to Peking. That evening, 340 marines and sailors arrived in the Legation Quarter. Four days later another 90 came in from Tientsin. These would be the last foreign troops to enter Peking until 14 August.

The Siege at Peking

On 9 June 1900 the first Boxer attack on foreign property in Peking occurred; the Racecourse was burned down. Sir Claude MacDonald, British minister in Peking and senior member of the foreign diplomatic corps, wasted no time in reacting to the sudden boldness of the Boxers. Without taking time to consult with the other ministers, he wired Admiral Seymour at Taku and requested him to advance on Peking with a sizeable relief force. On 10 June it became quite clear to the foreigners in the Legation Quarter that they would soon become the targets of the Boxer attacks. The telegraph line to Tientsin was cut. Regular mail service was halted. Chinese Imperial troops were seen openly collaborating with the Boxers. Chinese artillery was mounted along the city walls facing the Legation Quarter. It was announced on the 10th that a new head had been appointed to the Tsungli Yamen (the Chinese Foreign Office): that official was Prince Tuan—a noted pro-Boxer.

The situation worsened on the morning of the 11th when Mr Sugiyama, the Chancellor of the Japanese Legation, was murdered while on his way to the railway station to greet the expected Seymour relief column. The foreign ministers protested at the incident. The Chinese reported that the murder was the work of bandits and ruffians, choosing to cover up the true fact that General Tung Fu-hsiang's Imperial troops were involved. Foreigners and Chinese converts now fled to the two remaining concentrations of Westerners and Christians in Peking, the Legation Quarter and the Pei T'ang Cathedral. Unable to convince him to leave, the ministers had reluctantly allowed Bishop Favier to stay in

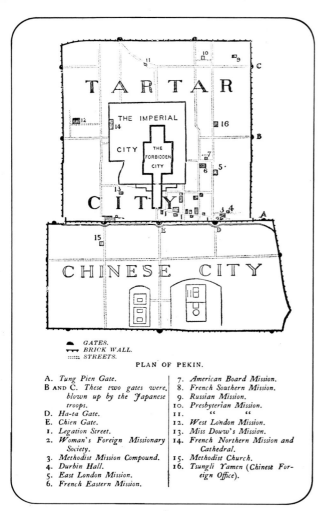

GATES.
BRICK WALL.
STREETS.

PLAN OF PEKIN.

A. *Tung Pien Gate.*	7. *American Board Mission.*
B AND C. *These two gates were,*	8. *French Southern Mission.*
blown up by the Japanese	9. *Russian Mission.*
troops.	10. *Presbyterian Mission.*
D. *Ha-ta Gate.*	11. " "
E. *Chien Gate.*	12. *West London Mission.*
1. *Legation Street.*	13. *Miss Douw's Mission.*
2. *Woman's Foreign Missionary*	14. *French Northern Mission and*
Society.	*Cathedral.*
3. *Methodist Mission Compound.*	15. *Methodist Church.*
4. *Durbin Hall.*	16. *Tsungli Yamen (Chinese For-*
5. *East London Mission.*	*eign Office).*
6. *French Eastern Mission.*	

Map showing the four cities of Peking, with some of the gates, government buildings, foreign missions and churches. All the churches except no. 14, the Pei T'ang Cathedral, were abandoned to the Chinese during the siege. The Legation Quarter is the area immediately above the section of wall bounded by the Chien (E) and Hata (D) Gates.

could no longer be guaranteed. The Chines offered safe conduct of the foreigners to Tientsi if they were ready to leave on the morning of th 20th.

The ministers met and unanimously agreed no to move. To stall for time they requested a audience with the Tsungli Yamen on the 20th but they received no reply. Finally, at 9.00am th German minister, Baron von Ketteler, could wai no longer, and with his interpreter set out for th Tsungli Yamen in two sedan chairs. Not far from the Legation Quarter, von Ketteler's chair wa stopped by an Imperial soldier who shot th German minister dead. The interpreter fled bac to the Legation Quarter and spread the news o von Ketteler's death. A note from the Chinese which arrived in the early afternoon, did no mention von Ketteler's murder, but instead requested the foreign ministers to reconsider th ultimatum of the previous day. The note wa ignored and at 4.00pm on 20 June 1900 th Chinese opened fire on the Legation Quarter.

A survey of the military forces available to th defence yielded the following totals:

Country	Officers	Me
Austria-Hungary	5	30
France	3	45
Germany	1	50
Great Britain	3	79
Italy	1	28
Japan	1	24
Russia	2	79
United States	3	53

There were also about seventy-five volunteers who had had some previous military experience. A second group of about fifty civilians, calling themselves 'Thornhill's Roughs', armed them selves with a curious assortment of sporting gun and hunting rifles and volunteered to serve on th barricades. Their amateur force became know as 'The Carving Knife Brigade' because of thei habit of lashing butcher knives onto the muzzle of their rifles as bayonets. At the Pei T'ang Cathedral were an Italian and a French office plus thirty French and eleven Italian sailors.

Artillery support consisted of an Austria Maxim gun, a British four-barrelled Nordenfeld gun, an Italian 1pdr. quick-firing gun and a American Colt machine gun. The Nordenfeld

the Pei T'ang with his followers, but they did send forty-three French and Italian sailors to assist in his defence.

By 16 June all foreigners and Chinese converts in Peking were either in the Legation Quarter or the Pei T'ang. On that same day the Boxers set fire to a large area of the Chinese city of Peking which contained stores and shops that dealt with foreigners. The fire destroyed over 4,000 businesses. Two tense but uneventful days followed the great fire; then, on 19 June, the ministers received an ultimatum from the Tsungli Yamen. The edict stated that all foreigners had to evacuate Peking within twenty-four hours or their safety

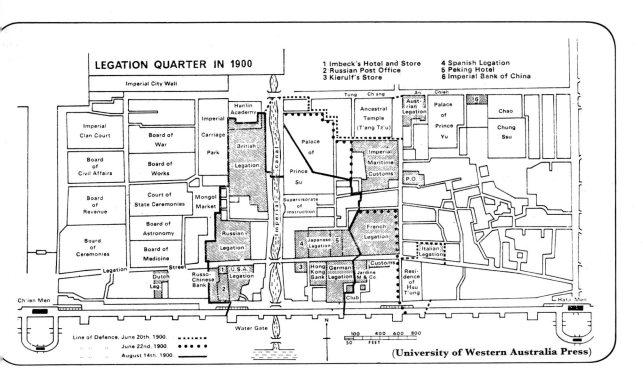

LEGATION QUARTER IN 1900

1 Imbeck's Hotel and Store 4 Spanish Legation
2 Russian Post Office 5 Peking Hotel
3 Kierulf's Store 6 Imperial Bank of China

Imperial City Wall

Imperial Clan Court
Board of War
Imperial Carriage Park
Hanlin Academy
Palace of Prince Su
Ancestral Temple (T'ang Tz'u)
Austrian Legation
Palace of Prince Yu
Chao Chung Ssu

Board of Civil Affairs
Board of Works
British Legation
Imperial Maritime Customs

Board of Revenue
Court of State Ceremonies
Mongol Market
Supervisorate of Instruction
French Legation

Board of Ceremonies
Board of Astronomy
Russian Legation
Japanese Legation
Italian Legation

Board of Medicine
Legation Street
Dutch Leg.
Russo-Chinese Bank
U.S.A. Legation
Hong Kong Bank
German Legation
Jardine M & Co.
Customs
Residence of Hsu T'ung
Club

Chien Men
Water Gate
Hata Men

Line of Defence, June 20th, 1900.
            June 22nd, 1900.
            August 14th, 1900.

100 400 600 800
50 FEET

(University of Western Australia Press)

was almost useless, since it jammed after every three or four rounds. The Russians had brought a supply of 9pdr. artillery shells to Peking, but they had left the cannon in Tientsin! The shells had to be dropped down a well to keep them from falling into the hands of the Chinese.

There were about 125 other foreign men in the Legations as well as 149 women and 79 children. Estimates placed the number of Chinese Christians in the Legation Quarter at about 2,700. Most of them had set up housekeeping in the grounds of Prince Su's Palace (the Su Wang Fu).

The Legation defenders made use of all available manpower. All foreigners with no military experience were organized into an array of committees. There were General, Fortification, Fuel, Sanitation, Water, Chinese Labour, Food Ration and Fire Defence Committees. A system of rations was organized, the most important of which were those of fresh meat, fruits and vegetables. Ample supplies of rice and canned goods were available at Imbeck's and Kierulf's stores. No food rations were organized for the Chinese within the perimeter. They survived during the siege by eating whatever they could find, including roots, plants, dogs, rats and garbage. Each day, all healthy Chinese men were required to work

A Russian barricade in the Legation Quarter of Peking, probably photographed toward the end of the siege; it is a considerable improvement over the early, flimsy barricades of carts and barrels. (University of Western Australia Press)

two hours for the general good. This work included strengthening the barricades, clearing rubble, digging countermines and grave digging.

The foreign women in the Legations also formed some committees of their own. Most notable were the volunteers who worked as nurses in the hospital and the 'sewing brigade'. Many of the ladies with sewing machines banded together and spent hours and hours sewing hundreds of sandbags for the barricades. The sandbags were made

British Royal Marines, a solitary 'bluejacket', and two US Marines with the garrison's Colt machine gun. (University of Western Australia Press)

from all sorts of materials: blankets, rice sacks, sheets and even fine multi-coloured silks.

On the 21st, Captain von Thomann of the Austro-Hungarian cruiser *Zenta* announced that he, as the senior officer among the Legation guards, was assuming overall military command. Less than a day later, von Thomann panicked during a heavy Chinese fusillade and ordered an immediate withdrawal from the outer perimeter to the British Legation compound—the final defence line. The ministers met in an emergency session and promptly relieved von Thomann of his command. Sir Claude MacDonald assumed military command. He immediately ordered everybody back to the original perimeter. The Chinese, caught off-guard, did not take advantage of the Allied withdrawal and were only able to burn the Italian Legation.

On the 23rd, the Chinese attempted to burn out the Legations by setting fire to the Mongol Market and the Hanlin College. Both fires burned out of control, but failed to spread into the Legations. The next day, the Allies decided that some offensive manoeuvres were needed. The Japanese laid a successful trap for the Chinese in the Su Wang Fu, and dozens of Boxers were killed in a vicious crossfire. The German Marines executed a devastating bayonet charge from their position against some crack Manchu Bannermen. All the Chinese were killed and the Germans left their bodies in the street as an example to the other Chinese. On the Tartar City Wall, a charge by US Marines cleared the wall of Chinese troops almost up to the Ch'ien Men.

Early July saw more offensive operations by the

Allies. On the 1st, a sortie by Japanese and Italian sailors disrupted Chinese positions beyond the Su Wang Fu. On the 3rd, fifty-four Americans, British and Russians attacked the Chinese position on the Tartar City Wall near the Ch'ien Men. The Chinese were routed and some banners, rifles and spears were captured.

On the afternoon of 7 July some Chinese Christians who were digging a trench came upon an old Anglo-French rifled cannon barrel dating from the 1860 expedition. The gun was removed and cleaned up by a couple of American Marines. By the next day it had been lashed onto a gun carriage supplied by the Italians. The Russian 9pdr. shells were fished out of the well, dried off and found to fit quite well into the cannon. The shells were disassembled and loaded as two separate charges through the muzzle. The cannon received many nicknames, including 'Boxer Bill', 'Old Betsy', 'Old Crock', and 'The Dowager Empress', but it seemed that 'The International Gun' best suited it. After all, it was an Anglo-French barrel on an Italian carriage firing Russian shells and was manned by two American gunners. For the remaining five weeks of the siege, 'The International Gun' served the Legation defenders faithfully.

In mid-July the newest threat to the Legations was Chinese mines. On the 13th, part of the French Legation was blown up by a mine. Several French sailors were killed, barricades were destroyed and a fire started. Countermines were begun at several points along the perimeter to prevent more Chinese underground attacks. On the 17th, a mysterious cease-fire descended upon the Legation Quarter of Peking. Soldiers of both sides took this opportunity to lay down their arms and chat! Cigarettes, fruit, candy and tea were exchanged and various matters were discussed. On the 18th, a message from Tientsin made it through the Chinese lines to the Japanese minister. The message stated that a combined Allied relief force of about 12,000 men was preparing to march on Peking. The news was met with many sighs of relief, but it would still be another month before Allied troops made their way into Peking.

The cease-fire continued until the 25th, when a sharp exchange of gunfire occurred over the Mongol Market. On 27 July another cease-fire

Group of Austro-Hungarian sailors, those on the left wearing the cap-tally of SMS *Zenta*. (National Army Museum)

was called and the Dowager Empress sent several carts bearing gifts of rice, fruit, melons and ice to the besieged foreigners! For the next week the guns were silent and all sorts of rumours found their way into the Legations, reporting various details of the Allied relief force.

Attacks against the Legations began again in earnest on 4 August. Fighting was extremely heavy around the Hanlin College, the Mongol Market and the Su Wang Fu. On the 12th and 13th, heavy fire-fights lasted all day and into the night. Early on 14 August, Maxim gunfire was heard outside the city. At 2.30pm a few men of the 7th Rajputs entered the Legation Quarter. They were quickly followed by the British General Gaselee and his staff. The Peking Legations had been relieved, after a siege of fifty-five days.

If the situation in the Legation Quarter was bad, that in the Pei T'ang Cathedral was hopeless. Bishop Favier had almost 3,900 people in the grounds of the North Cathedral (as the Pei T'ang was also known) of whom only forty-three were armed. There was little food, and no fresh meat or fruit. Luckily, there was an adequate supply of water from the Cathedral's wells. It was a miracle that the Pei T'ang held out—a miracle which was undoubtedly aided by Bishop Favier's spiritual leadership and the courage of the forty-three French and Italian sailors who were the Cathedral's only armed defenders.

As many as 2,000 Boxers and Imperial troops assaulted the Cathedral's defences, but they could not overwhelm the defenders. On one day, fourteen Chinese artillery pieces fired over 400 shells into the grounds of the church. The excellent rifle fire of the French and Italian sailors was one major contributing factor to the solid defence. Two volleys, totalling fifty-eight rounds, fired at one mass charge by Boxers left forty-three dead Chinese attackers on the ground in front of the barricades!

The Chinese dug and exploded four mines during their siege of the Pei T'ang. All of the mines were detonated along the north end of the Cathedral grounds, where the foundling hospital was located. Many of the dead were Chinese children and infants. One nun lost all sixty-six of the children who were under her care during the explosion of just one mine.

On 30 July Lt. Henry, the French officer, was killed, and Lt. Olivieri, the Italian officer, took command. Olivieri was in the hospital at the time of the largest mine explosion on 12 August and was buried under tons of rubble. He was dug out two hours later, and found to be alive. During the next four days the Chinese attacks diminished, and on 16 August a combined relief force of French, British and Russian troops cleared the area around the Pei T'ang, only to find that the Japanese had already relieved the Cathedral. For Bishop Favier and more than 3,000 people in the church grounds, the fifty-seven-day ordeal was over.

After the relief of the Pei T'ang, a survey of casualties among the defenders was taken:

The civilian casualties include Sugiyama and von Ketteler. No records were kept of casualties among the Chinese Christians, but they numbered at least several hundred and possibly as many as one thousand.

Seymour's Expedition

It was 11.30pm on 9 June before Admiral Sir Edward Seymour, Commander-in-Chief of the British China Station, received Sir Claude MacDonald's request for help. Seymour immediately began organizing a column for the advance. The Admiral left Taku with a contingent of Royal Marines and bluejackets at 6.00am on the 10th, and marched to Tientsin.

Once in Tientsin, Seymour began preparations for an immediate advance on Peking. He hoped to make the journey by train, so he asked the foreign consuls in Tientsin to make arrangements with Yu Lu, Governor-General of Chihli Province,

| | Military Personnel | | Civilians | |
Country	Killed	Wounded	Killed	Wounded
Austria-Hungary	4	11	–	–
France	16	45	2	6
Germany	12	15	1	1
Great Britain	3	20	3	6
Italy	13	16	–	–
Japan	5	20	5	8
Russia	4	19	1	1
United States	7	10	–	1

o allow the trains to leave Tientsin. While the consuls were negotiating with Yu, Seymour assembled his force at the railway station. The relief column contained just over 2,100 men as follows: 915 British, 512 Germans, 312 Russians, 157 French, 111 Americans, 54 Japanese, 42 Italians and 26 Austrians. Artillery support consisted of seven field guns and ten machine guns.

By 9.30am permission had been secured for the five special trains to leave Tientsin. In arranging the trains, Seymour drew on relevant British experience in Egypt and South Africa. Preceding each locomotive was a flat car or gondola car protected with boiler plates, sandbags or heavy timbers. This car carried a machine gun and twenty to thirty infantrymen. Following the locomotive were some passenger coaches carrying troops, and other freight cars carrying artillery, ammunition and supplies. Each train also contained one car with rail, ties and tools for making repairs to any damaged sections of track which might be encountered.

Admiral Seymour expected to be in Peking before the end of the day, so he only loaded rations for three days. No explanation exists as to why Seymour felt so confident of an easy advance to Peking. The expedition had to travel almost 100 miles on a rail line whose condition was unknown, through territory infested with hostile Boxers. Reliable intelligence also placed General Nieh Shih-ch'eng's Chinese Imperial Army somewhere between Seymour and his goal. Seymour hoped that General Nieh's European trained and armed force would be fighting against the Boxers, as General Yüan Shi-K'ai's imperial troops were doing in northern Shantung Province. The Allies felt confident that they could deal with any Boxers whom they might meet, but were apprehensive about fighting both the Boxers and the Chinese Imperial Army.

The column had not reached Peking by the end of the first day. Admiral Seymour's force had advanced only twenty-five miles, to Yang Tsun, before encountering badly damaged tracks. The rest of the day was spent repairing the line. On the 11th the relief column pressed on, and by nightfall the trains pulled into Lang Fang, about forty miles from Peking. There they encountered

a force of Boxers who were destroying the tracks. The enemy were dispersed, and repairs began. A scouting force was sent ahead, but could get no further than the village of An Ting, about ten miles along the tracks, because of strong Boxer resistance.

Admiral Seymour's supplies for repairing the tracks, as well as his rations, were running low, so he decided to wait in Lang Fang while a train was sent back to Tientsin for more supplies. On the 15th the supply train returned to Lang Fang, empty. Boxer activity between Lang Fang and Yang Tsun was heavy, and the tracks had been effectively put out of service for their entire length from Yang Tsun to Tientsin. Seymour had no choice but to pull back. The trains withdrew towards Yang Tsun at a very slow rate. On the 18th, German cavalry scouts returned to the trains to report that they had skirmished with Chinese Imperial troops, who seemed to have joined forces with the Boxers. This news was devastating for Seymour.

On the 19th the trains reached the river near Yang Tsun. The bridge in front of them was badly damaged and unsafe to cross. The troops detrained and began to march the rest of the way to Tientsin along the Pei Ho. Some junks were captured to help transport the wounded and artillery downstream. The river level was still low and the junks were continually running aground.

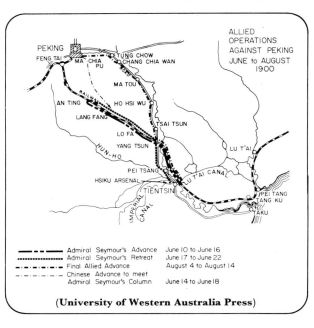

(University of Western Australia Press)

Finally, the artillery had to be dumped overboard in order to lighten the loads of the junks.

On 22 June, after three days of very slow progress, the column came upon a government building with a very weak guard of Chinese troops. A decision was made to attack, and after only a few minutes of fighting Admiral Seymour discovered that he had captured the Imperial Chinese Arsenal at Hsiku, not far from Tientsin. Supplies of food, water, arms and ammunition were found in the arsenal. Seymour decided to hold his force at Hsiku and wait for help from Tientsin. The relief force remained at Hsiku on half rations until the 26th, when they were rescued by a force of Russian Cossacks. The first attempt to relieve Peking had failed miserably.

Taku and Tientsin

After Admiral Seymour's force had left Tientsin, the other Allied admirals off the Taku bar held a conference. At the meeting the commanders voted not to land any additional troops. They felt that any more foreign troops on Chinese soil would only escalate a situation which they would prefer to keep under control.

Mid-June brought several disturbing reports which caused the admirals to meet again to reconsider their earlier decision. On 15 June the Boxers took control of the native city of Tientsin. Boxer pressure on the rest of Tientsin, including the International Settlement, was increasing at an alarming rate. All Allied strategists agreed that Tientsin was needed as a base for any major operations against Peking. Of possibly greater concern was the fact that nothing had been heard from Admiral Seymour's force for over a week. The telegraph line to Peking had been cut for nine days. Rumours of Baron von Ketteler's murder had reached the coast, and there was no way to confirm the stories with the ministers in Peking. On the 16th, rumours of the events at Peking appeared to be confirmed by a reliable news agency. The world press snatched up the story, and news of the situation in Peking made the front pages of major newspapers in Europe and America. (It is interesting to note that the world press reported von Ketteler's murder fou[r] days before it actually happened!) The Allie[s] also observed Chinese vessels laying mines at th[e] entrance to the Pei Ho, and Chinese troop[s] seizing the railway near Taku. The Chines[e] government was apparently preparing to bloc[k] the Allied route inland.

Late on the 16th, the Allied naval commander[s] held a hasty meeting on board the flagship of th[e] Russian admiral. The situation at Taku an[d] Tientsin was discussed and they decided to tak[e] immediate action in order to secure the rout[e] inland. A daring and ingenious plan was devise[d] to bombard, storm and capture the forts guardin[g] the Taku bar from the landward side. An officia[l] letter was drafted by the admirals and sent to th[e] Chinese officials at Taku. The letter was signed b[y] all the Allied admirals except the America[n] commander, Rear-Admiral Kempff, whose hand[s] were tied by a directive from Washingto[n] forbidding him from participating in any hostil[e] actions against the Chinese. The letter stated tha[t] the Allies intended to occupy the Taku forts b[y] 2.00am on the 17th with or without the permissio[n] of the Chinese authorities.

A fleet of eight shallow-draught gunboats an[d] two destroyers was assembled and a stormin[g] party of 900 marines and sailors was distribute[d] among them. The American representative, th[e] gunboat *Monocacy*, did not actually take part i[n] the attack (due to Admiral Kempff's orders). Th[e] little flotilla moved across the bar and entered th[e] Pei Ho unopposed to take up positions above th[e] forts. The Taku forts had recently been rebuilt an[d] rearmed with the most modern Krupp coasta[l] artillery, but the big guns could only be fired ou[t] to sea. The Allies were well aware of this whe[n] they decided to attack the forts from upriver wit[h] only small, unarmoured gunboats. About an hou[r] before the Allied ultimatum expired, the Chines[e] commander of the forts gave the Allies hi[s] answer—the guns opened fire on the foreig[n] gunboats. Six of the gunboats moved downstrea[m] and began firing in return on the forts.

At 3.00am the Allied assault force was pu[t] ashore on the mud flats near the North-West For[t.] Sailors and marines from seven nations bega[n] working their way into position for the fir[st] assault against the Chinese positions. Firin[g] continued between the forts and the gunboats until daylight. The early morning light must have helped Allied gunnery, as two magazines were blown up and several Chinese guns were knocked off their mounts. At 6.00am a bayonet charge by the Allied troops captured the North-West Fort. The North Fort was taken by storm a few minutes later. The other two Chinese forts ran up white flags and surrendered. The Allies had secured the way to Tientsin and Peking at the cost of 172 casualties. None of the gunboats had suffered any serious damage.

The Allied actions at Taku must have had some influence on China's decision to commit Imperial troops to the fighting. Admiral Seymour's relief force was certainly attacked by General Nieh's troops as a result of the Allied actions at Taku. The ultimatum given to the foreign ministers at Peking by the Tsungli Yamen on the 19th was also directly related to the capture of the Taku forts.

Finally, on 21 June, the Chinese government officially declared war on the Allies.

★ ★ ★

Estimates put the number of Chinese in and around Tientsin at 10,000, including Imperial troops with at least 60 modern artillery pieces. The defenders of Tientsin had only 2,400 men and nine artillery pieces to cover a perimeter which was almost five miles long. On 15 June large bands of Boxers ran through much of Tientsin setting fire to foreign buildings. The fires were accompanied by the chanting of 'sha, sha' ('kill, kill').

An exceptionally sound and well-planned system of defensive positions was built under the guidance of a young American engineer, Herbert Hoover, who would become President of the United States twenty-nine years later. Many of the barricades, especially along the river, were

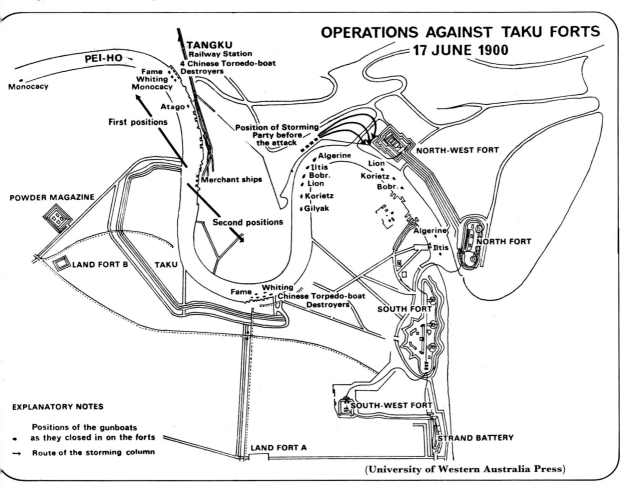

OPERATIONS AGAINST TAKU FORTS 17 JUNE 1900

PEI-HO

TANGKU Railway Station 4 Chinese Torpedo-boat Destroyers

Fame Whiting Monocacy

Monocacy

Atago

First positions

Position of Storming Party before the attack

Merchant ships

POWDER MAGAZINE

Algerine

Iltis
Bobr.
Lion
Korietz
Gilyak

Lion
Korietz
Bobr.

NORTH-WEST FORT

Second positions

Algerine

Iltis

NORTH FORT

LAND FORT B   **TAKU**

Fame   Whiting
Chinese Torpedo-boat Destroyers

SOUTH FORT

SOUTH-WEST FORT

EXPLANATORY NOTES

Positions of the gunboats as they closed in on the forts

Route of the storming column

LAND FORT A

STRAND BATTERY

(University of Western Australia Press)

Austrian and German sailors storming the North-West Fort at Taku, 17 June 1900. *(Illustrated London News)*

made from huge sacks of grain found in the Chinese warehouses along the Pei Ho. Trenches and artillery positions were dug and barricades were thrown up across key streets. The foreign women and children were gathered together and moved into the cellar of the Municipal Hall, as it seemed to be the most artillery-proof shelter available.

On the morning of 17 June, an all-out assault by Chinese Imperial troops and Boxers was launched against the International Settlement. Even while the Allied troops were 'mopping up' at the Taku forts, the 2,400-man defence force at Tientsin was being severely pressed on all sides by the Chinese. The perimeter held, however, due to the excellent defensive positions which had been constructed by Hoover. During the attack the telegraph line to Taku was cut, so the victorious Allied forces on the coast knew nothing of the situation in Tientsin.

On the 20th, the Chinese attacks on Tientsin slackened. An Englishman, James Watts, and three Cossacks made a dash on horseback through the Chinese lines to Taku to inform the Allied admirals of the desperate situation in Tientsin. An advance force of 500 men was immediately sent towards the besieged International Settlement. The column advanced to within about four miles of Tientsin before being turned back. A large contingent of troops, numbering almost 8,000, broke through the Chinese lines and entered Tientsin on 23 June.

The relief of Tientsin forced the Chinese Imperial troops to fall back to Peking. The relaxation of organized Chinese military pressure allowed the Allies to send out search parties for Admiral Seymour. On the 26th, a reconnaissance in force by Cossacks found the British admiral and the Allied troops at Hsiku. Seymour and his men finally made their way back into Tientsin sixteen days after they had originally left on a 'one-day' train trip to Peking. Once Seymour's force had rested, the Allies felt confident about taking the offensive. Two-thirds of Tientsin was still occupied by Boxers; they had to be eliminated or dispersed before any operations against Peking could be attempted.

During the next week both sides began building their forces for the coming battle of Tientsin. The Chinese Imperial troops returned and reoccupied the Hsiku Arsenal. The arsenal at Tientsin was destroyed by Allied forces on 27 June. A force of Japanese troops drove the Chinese from the Tientsin Racecourse early in July. Thanks to this manoeuvre, the Allies were able to attack and destroy the Hsiku Arsenal on 9 July. The Chinese, now short of ammunition and arms, began to waver and crumble under the Allied offensive.

On the 13th, 5,000 foreign troops attacked the native city of Tientsin. The fighting was intense. For the first time the Chinese were putting up a stiff resistance to the Allied assaults. In the past they had usually abandoned their positions and withdrawn when they were out-flanked or out-gunned; now, many of them fought until all hope was lost. Casualties on both sides were heavy during the day and a half of fighting. Finally, on

the 14th, the Chinese took flight and the Allies gained control of the whole of Tientsin.

The loss of Tientsin constituted much more than just a lost battle for the Chinese. They were now deprived of two of their largest arsenals in northern China, and control of the railway to the coast. An even greater blow to the Imperial forces was the death of General Nieh Shih-ch'eng. Some reports state that the general was killed in battle by exposing himself unnecessarily to Allied artillery fire; other statements suggest that he committed suicide. In either case, it seems likely that General Nieh had 'lost face' in being defeated. It seems probable that he chose to 'save face' and die in battle, or by his own hand, rather than report his defeat to the Imperial Court.

The Relief of Peking

After Tientsin had been secured, the Allies chose to sit back and regroup. Reports of a massacre in Peking were felt to be accurate, so the foreign troops thought that they had no reason to rush forward and lift the siege. As a repeat of the Seymour disaster was undesirable, a large force, able to hold its lines of communication, was deemed necessary. In Europe, the International Relief Force was organized and the Kaiser convinced the Allied representatives that a German should be named as Supreme Commander. General Albrecht Graf von Waldersee was chosen by the Kaiser. Von Waldersee had been very popular as Chief of the German General Staff between 1888 and 1891 and this, coupled with his diplomatic charm and 'man of the world' reputation, made him an excellent choice. A call for volunteers went out from Berlin and, early in August, von Waldersee and the 'East Asia Brigade' sailed from Wilhelmshaven.

In China, however, efforts to relieve Peking had been renewed. Late in July a messenger had made his way through the Chinese lines and informed the Allies in Tientsin that the Peking Legations were still in foreign hands. Immediate relief was needed as food and ammunition supplies were

James Watts, the Englishman whose ride from Tientsin to Taku may have saved the International Settlement. He wears the scarlet jacket of the Tientsin Volunteers, the collar and cuffs trimmed with white. The blue breeches have scarlet belts. The brass cypher 'T.V.C.' is worn on the khaki slouch hat and the jacket shoulder-straps. It is not known if Watts wore this uniform during his epic ride. (Major A. McK. Annand)

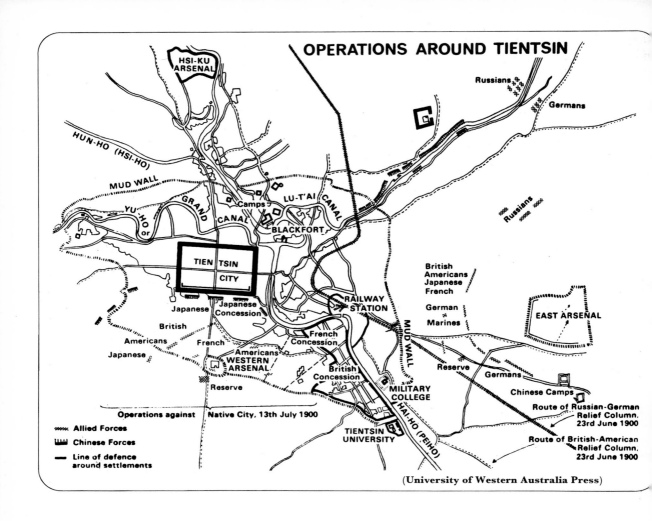

OPERATIONS AROUND TIENTSIN

HSI-KU ARSENAL

Russians

Germans

HUN-HO (HSI-HO)

MUD WALL

Camps

LU-T'AI CANAL

Russians

GRAND CANAL

YU-HO or

BLACKFORT

TIEN TSIN CITY

British
Americans
Japanese
French

German

Marines

EAST ARSENAL

RAILWAY STATION

Japanese Concession

Japanese

British

Americans

French

French Concession

Americans
WESTERN ARSENAL

Japanese

British Concession

Reserve

Germans

Chinese Camps

Reserve

MUD WALL

MILITARY COLLEGE

HAI-HO (PEIHO)

Route of Russian-German Relief Column, 23rd June 1900

Operations against | Native City, 13th July 1900

Route of British-American Relief Column, 23rd June 1900

TIENTSIN UNIVERSITY

Allied Forces
Chinese Forces
Line of defence around settlements

(University of Western Australia Press)

running low. All carts, wagons and other vehicles as well as draught animals in and around Tientsin were gathered up to be used as the supply train for the new relief force. On 3 August the Allied generals held a meeting and decided to move out on the 5th.

With Graf von Waldersee still at sea somewhere between Wilhelmshaven and Taku, the Allied forces needed an interim commander. The generals chose British General Alfred Gaselee to command the second relief column. The Allies surprised themselves by finishing their preparations on the 4th; as a result the column was able to move out a day earlier than planned. The force numbered about 20,000 men as follows: 10,000 Japanese, 4,000 Russians, 3,000 British, 2,000 Americans, 800 French, 200 Germans, 58 Austrians and 53 Italians. There were 70 artillery pieces and machine guns with the column.

The force would follow the Pei Ho north from Tientsin, using the river as an artery of supply; the supply column of wagons and carts would be supplemented by a fleet of junks carrying food and ammunition. Conditions during the march were almost unbearable. There was no wind, not a cloud in the sky, and daytime temperatures reached as high as 104°F. The roads had turned to a sea of choking dust.

Cavalry scouts reported that the Chinese were regrouping and preparing to stand their ground at Pei Tsang, a town on the railway about seven miles north of Tientsin. Just after 4.00am on 5 August the battle of Pei Tsang began. Within an hour the first Chinese trenches had been captured. Before noon the town and all its defences were in Allied hands and the Chinese army was in flight. The majority of the fighting was done by the Japanese and the Russians, but a battery of Royal

Navy 12pdrs. (courtesy of Captain Percy Scott and HMS *Terrible*, fresh from the Boer War) offered excellent support.

On the 6th the Chinese attempted to regroup and offer battle at Yang Tsun, ten miles further up the road. Standing again behind a good system of trenches and earthworks, the Chinese troops hoped to halt the Allied advance. This time the Americans and the British led the assault. Many men collapsed under the weight of their packs in the extreme heat; yet still they advanced on the Chinese lines. Miraculously the Allies captured one trench after another. The Allies had control of Yang Tsun by nightfall.

The next Allied objective was the walled city of Tungchow, about twenty miles further to the north. The advance through the heat and dust was very slow. Chinese resistance was virtually non-existent. The only real excitement came from the regular attempts of the Russians to advance past the Japanese in the race towards Peking. In the early morning hours of 12 August, the Japanese vanguard reached the walls of Tungchow. Some guns were brought up and the South Gate was blown down. The Japanese entered a deserted city: the Imperial troops had been withdrawn, leaving the town to the Boxers. The Boxers had run amok—killing, looting and burning—before they, too, had fled.

The relief column halted in Tungchow and the Allied generals held a conference on the evening of the 12th. It was decided to scout ahead and try to send cavalry as close to Peking as possible. General Gaselee wanted the final advance on Peking to be a well-planned and executed military manoeuvre. He hoped that the last twelve miles to Peking would not be marred by any glory-seeking by members of the Allied force, especially the highly competitive Japanese and Russians.

The plan of attack against Peking envisaged a co-ordinated assault against four of the gates in Peking's city wall. The Russians would attack the Tung Chih Men ('Men' meaning gate). The Americans would assault the Tung Pien Men, the Japanese the Chi Hua Men and the British the Sha Huo Men. The assault would begin on the morning of 15 August. Each contingent would march to their zone of deployment and then wait

Royal Marines, a US Marine and a sailor pose with the 'International Gun' devised by the garrison during the siege. (University of Western Australia Press)

for the predetermined time to launch the attack. On the 13th, the Russian cavalry scouts returned to report that they had been able to advance to within a few hundred yards of the Peking city wall. The Allied generals held a hasty meeting and, in view of the reports of the Cossacks, voted to move up the assault on Peking by twenty-four hours.

By the night of the 13th, all of the Allied troops were in position and bivouacking for the night. The Russians did not set up camp, however, and were on the move towards Peking before midnight. It appeared as if the Russians were not going to co-operate in the co-ordinated attack, but rather were making a race for the honour of being the first of the Allies to enter Peking and relieve the foreign Legations.

To complicate the situation further, the Russians did not attack their assigned gate. During their night march they moved obliquely across the Allied front and assaulted the Tung Pien Men, which was the American objective. The Russian attack was not very successful. By morning they had only managed to force the outer of the two gates in the structure and were able to occupy only a small portion of the city wall.

The Americans, reacting to the premature move by the Russians, broke camp and began advancing at daybreak. General Yamaguchi, fearful that General Linivitch's Russians would steal the show, also moved out at daybreak with his Japanese forces. General Gaselee, seeing his well-planned assault disintegrate before his eyes, could do nothing but order a general advance immediately. All thought of a co-ordinated attack on Peking was abandoned.

General Chaffee's Americans, now with no gate to attack, chose to assault the actual city wall between the Sha Huo Men and the Tung Pien Men. Upon reaching the wall, the US troops were faced with a problem: how to scale a thirty-foot-high masonry wall without scaling ladders or grappling hooks? A young bugler from the Fourteenth Infantry, Calvin P. Titus, came forward and volunteered to climb the wall. Titus worked his way to the top, unarmed, and found this particular section of the wall unmanned! Another man followed with a rope and soon there were about twenty men on top of the wall. At 11.03am the Stars and Stripes were unfurled on top of the wall and a cheer went up from the entire US contingent. An improvised ladder made of bamboo poles was put to use and, by noon, there were enough Americans on the wall for an attack to help out the Russians. Once the Chinese found that they had been out-flanked, they fled, and the Tung Pien gate was cleared. For his actions, Bugler Titus was awarded the Congressional Medal of Honor.

A little after noon the British began their assault on the Sha Huo Men. Resistance was minimal as the Royal Artillery blasted a hole in the gate. Marching almost unopposed up to the wall outside the Legations, the British could see three Allied flags still flying. For a brief moment, General Gaselee thought he was too late; then a sailor appeared on top of the wall and signalled the relievers to enter via the sluice gate on the Imperial Drainage Canal. Some men from the 7th Rajputs broke down the bars over the gate from the outside while several US Marines did the same on the inside. Just after 2.30pm on 14 August 1900, British troops entered the Legation Quarter and lifted the fifty-five-day siege.

What of the other Allies? At the Tung Pien Men there was quite a traffic jam as both the Russian and American columns attempted to enter Peking. Heavy street fighting also slowed the advance of the US and Russian troops. General Chaffee, followed closely by the American troops

and the Russians, marched into the Legation Quarter at about 4.30pm, only to find that the British had preceded them by about two hours. Where were the Japanese? With their usual exuberance, the Japanese contingent had decided to not only attack the Chi Hua Men, which had been assigned to them, but also to attack the Tung Chih Men, which had been abandoned by the Russians. This decision slowed the Japanese advance and it was late in the evening before the first Japanese troops made their way down Legation Street.

Early in the morning of 15 August the Dowager Empress, part of the Imperial family and a few retainers fled from Peking. They fled to the south where the pro-Manchu forces were strongest. Tzu Hsi ordered General Jung Lu, Hsu Tung, Kang I and Chang I to stay in Peking to form some sort of interim government. She also hoped that they could begin negotiations with the Allies. Many members of the Court died or were killed during the night of 14–15 August. The Emperor's favourite wife was thrown down a well at Tzu Hsi's orders. Hsu Tung, despite his orders to stay in Peking to form a government, hung himself. After several days of flight it was decided that the Imperial Court should set itself up at Sian, capital of Shansi Province, about 700 miles south-west of Peking. The journey was long and slow, but Tzu Hsi, the Emperor and their small contingent finally arrived at Sian on 26 October.

At first light on the morning of 15 August, General Chaffee ordered the American troops up for an assault against the Forbidden City. US troops moved with little opposition up to the gate in the Forbidden City wall. A section of the 6th Artillery was deployed; the lieutenant commanding walked up to the gate and marked a large 'X' in the centre of it with a piece of chalk, and the guns opened fire. After only two rounds the gate was blown open and the 14th US Infantry entered the Imperial Palace grounds.

Once they had entered the Forbidden City the Americans encountered rather strong Chinese resistance. The entrance to the Imperial Palace grounds seemed to be a series of courtyards, one after another. Each time the Americans entered one they would find themselves facing concentrated Chinese fire from three sides. Slowly and

Scene inside a Chinese arsenal near Tientsin, possibly the Hsiku Arsenal. Officers of the Imperial forces can be recognized by their swords, and the lavish embroidery of their jackets. Note the 'Mandarin' hats worn by nearly all of these troops. (US National Archives)

methodically, the US troops worked their way towards their objective, Tzu Hsi's Palace. Soon there was but one more courtyard separating the Americans from the Palace. Then came the order to halt and withdraw.

The American troops were astonished. They had fought for most of the morning, fifteen men had been killed and scores wounded, and for what? An order to withdraw just before reaching their objective? It didn't make sense. A Franco-Russian protest to the other Allied commanders and ministers had convinced the Allies to put a halt to Chaffee's unauthorized assault. Chaffee was ordered back 'in the best interest of all the Allied powers'. The Americans, including Chaffee, were outraged, but could do nothing but withdraw without jeopardizing peace among the Allies.

Peking was divided up among the Allies into zones in which each power had the authority to act as police. Chinese attempts to set up an interim government disintegrated into anarchy. The Allies spent most of their time looting or defending against looters. The American and British troops were strictly forbidden to take part in any looting. The Russians, French, Germans and Japanese,

however, felt it was their right, as victors, to sack Peking. The city was stripped of much of its art objects, gold and silver. Even the ancient astronomical instruments at the Peking observatory were packed up and carted off to Europe.

After the American assault on 15 August, the Forbidden City lay untouched until the 28th. On the 27th, the Allied ministers and generals had decided to hold a 'victory march' through the Forbidden City on the following day. Each of the eight powers sent contingents of soldiers, sailors and marines. The commanding general, foreign minister and a group of the Legation defenders accompanied each country's detachment. There was no interference from the Chinese. The occupation of Peking was now complete.

After Peking

The relief of the Peking Legations did not mark an end to the campaigning against the Boxers. Throughout September and into October expeditions were launched to break up the remaining concentrations of Boxer strength. Small actions were fought around Peking and Tientsin, at Patachow, Pao Ting Fu and in other areas of

British 'bluejackets' posing with a Nordenfeldt gun from HMS Orlando; Tientsin, 1900. (Courtesy John Fabb/B. T. Batsford Ltd.)

northern China. Most saw the Allies advancing to the Chinese position, firing one or two volleys, and the Chinese fleeing into the local countryside.

At Patachow, a joint Anglo-American force under the command of American Major-General James H. Wilson was sent out to disperse a sizeable force of Boxers. The insurgents were gathered around a group of pagodas known as the Eight Temples. The Allied force, 2,000 strong, spent less than two hours in action. The Boxers were routed and sent fleeing into the hills by a well-executed flanking manoeuvre.

A number of other small actions occurred around Peking and Tientsin. An example of this sort of action was fought at Chang Ping Chow on 4 September. Troop 'L' of the 6th US Cavalry contacted some Chinese Imperial troops near the Great Wall on the caravan route to Mongolia about thirty miles north-west of Peking. A few shots were exchanged and the Chinese fled.

General von Waldersee and the East Asia Brigade arrived off Taku on 21 September. The Allies had finally got their Commander-in-Chief. Von Waldersee moved to Peking, where a review of the Allied troops was held in his honour. He immediately requested that peace negotiations be initiated by the Allied ministers. The final Boxer stronghold, Pao Ting Fu, would be dealt with personally by von Waldersee and a joint Allied expedition headed up by the recently-arrived East Asia Brigade.

By mid-October the Allied force was organized and moved out of Peking. The advance to Pao Ting Fu was unopposed. The heavy concentration of Boxers turned out to be an unorganized mob which had locked itself in the city. General Gaselee attempted to negotiate a surrender of the city. The Chinese refused to give up so the Allies were forced to attack. On 20 October, the last major centre of Boxer resistance was captured by he Allies. Von Waldersee ordered the town to be sacked and put to the torch as a 'punishment'.

A series of war crimes trials was held, hundreds of Chinese being brought before a military commission containing representatives from all eight of the Allied powers. Chinese officials, military leaders and Boxers by the hundreds were tried, and most were put to death. Huge fines were levied against many cities to help pay for the Allied expeditions. A fine of 100,000 *taels* (the exchange rate for the *tael* in 1900 was officially set at three shillings and one penny sterling) was levied against Pao Ting Fu. In addition to this fine, the contents of the Pao Ting Fu Treasury, about 240,000 *taels*, was divided up among the Allies. Most walled Chinese cities had their towers destroyed and their gates dismantled. Weapons and ammunition were gathered up and destroyed.

Towards the end of September, China's two official peace negotiators had been nominated and accepted by the Allies. It was hoped that Li Hung-chang and Prince Ch'ing would be able to negotiate the best of all possible deals with the Allied representatives. Li had been active in Chinese diplomacy since 1871. Prince Ch'ing had been President of the Tsungli Yamen from 1884 to 10 June 1900, when he was replaced by Prince Tuan.

The Allied representatives at the peace talks were the ministers of the eight military powers which had been involved in the fighting, plus the ministers from the Netherlands, Belgium and Spain. Of the ministers who had been besieged at Peking, all but one took part in the negotiations. The notable exception was Sir Claude MacDonald, who was replaced by Sir Ernest Satew, Britain's representative in Tokyo. Sir Claude was dealt a heavy personal blow by this decision, but care was taken in London to see that he was not dishonoured, and he left Peking a hero.

The Allies were not prepared to be lenient with the Chinese. Even before Peking had been taken, agreement had been reached on three points which would be considered as 'non-negotiable'. Responsible Chinese officials and Boxers were to be punished. China would have to pay the costs of the Allied military expedition. All existing treaties between China and the Allies would have to be renegotiated. By November, nine more points were agreed by the Allies. China had to send a special envoy to Berlin to apologize for Baron von Ketteler's murder, and a monument to the murdered diplomat must be erected in Peking. A similar mission had to be sent to Tokyo with regard to Mr Sugiyama's death. Areas where foreigners were killed were not allowed to have Civil Service tests for five years; this was a serious punishment directed at Chinese officials and scholars. Monuments were to be erected in foreign and Chinese Christian cemeteries which had been desecrated by the Boxers. China was forbidden to import arms or war material for two years. The Taku forts were to be disarmed and levelled. A defence line was to be built around the Legation Quarter in Peking, and Chinese citizens would be forbidden to reside within the perimeter. The Allies would be allowed to garrison the lines of communication between Peking and the coast. Imperial edicts were to be distributed which declared that hostility to foreigners was a crime punishable by death and that local officials would be held personally responsible for the safety of foreigners within their provinces. Finally, the Tsungli Yamen was to be abolished and replaced by a more modern foreign office.

These draconian demands were all agreed upon by the Allies and were set out in a document which was sent to the Chinese officials on 22 December 1900. This was not presented to the Imperial court as a treaty, but instead as a 'suggestion'. The Allies knew that the Manchus would never sign such a document as it would signify a serious 'loss of face'. Rather, the ministers hoped that the Chinese would take the suggestions in hand and issue a series of official edicts which would meet all of the Allies' demands.

As early as September of 1900, some of the Allied demands had been partially met by Chinese decrees. High officials who had been involved with the Boxers, such as Prince Tuan, were punished by removal from office. The Allies demanded more than removal from office: they wanted executions. Tzu Hsi could not order the execution of any member of the Imperial Court, but she did banish Prince Tuan and his brother, Tsai Lan, to western China for life. The Governor of Shansi, Yu Hsien, was executed along with

Ying Nien and Hsu Cheng-yu. Chao Shu-chiao, Prince Chang and other high-ranking officials were allowed to commit suicide. Kang I, Hsu Tung, Li Peng-heng and others who were already dead were posthumously dishonoured.

In late December 1900, an official decree informed local Chinese officials that they would be held responsible for the lives of all foreigners within their areas. On 1 February 1901 the Boxer Society, the Big Sword Society, and other anti-foreign societies were officially dissolved and 'anti-foreignism' was declared a crime punishable by death. On 29 May 1901 the Chinese offered to pay the Allies an indemnity of 450 million *taels* (£67.5 million sterling), payable over thirty-one years at 4 per cent interest. The Tsungli Yamen was abolished on 24 July 1901, and was replaced by a more modern foreign office, the Wai Wu Pu. Delegations were sent to Berlin and Tokyo to apologize for the deaths of von Ketteler and Sugiyama. China prohibited the import of arms for two years beginning on 29 August. Other decrees in regard to the Legation defences, Allied peace-keeping troops, erection of monuments in cemeteries and the razing of the Taku forts followed.

In view of the fact that Imperial edicts, which for the most part met the Allied demands, had been issued, the official Peace Protocol of Peking was signed by the Allied and Chinese representatives on 7 September 1901, officially ending the Boxer Rebellion. Throughout 1901 the Allied armies had been trickling out of China. Only the Germans remained in strength. Typical of the Allied contingents which remained was that of the United States—one regiment of infantry, a squadron of cavalry and a battery of artillery.

Early in 1902 the Dowager Empress returned to the Imperial Palace in the Forbidden City. Her journey from Sian took nearly two and a half months, and was accompanied by much pomp, ceremony and dignity. Tzu Hsi arrived to find much of Peking in ruins, but she was pleased to find the Forbidden City intact. She was also pleased to find most of her personal treasure still untouched where it had been buried by her eunuchs in August 1900.

The Dowager Empress was quick to make herself accessible to the foreign ministers. Several

The Dowager Empress, Tzu Hsi. (US National Archives)

formal and informal meetings were held. Many of the treaties were negotiated and signed under the consenting eyes of the Empress. Tzu Hsi personally apologized to many of the ministers and their wives for the hardships they had suffered during the siege. For the final eight years of her reign, the Dowager Empress appeared to be attempting to redeem herself in foreign eyes.

★   ★   ★

The Boxer Rebellion was a heavy blow to China's world prestige. Her defeat by Japan in 1894-95 had already placed her second among Asian powers, and defeat at the hands of the Allies lowered her standing even further. Though never considered as the single cause, the Boxer Rebellion was a contributing factor to the eventual fall of the Manchu Dynasty in 1912. China's army had proved to be ill-equipped, poorly trained and incompetently led. She was virtually forced to sign a multitude of treaties which gave concession after concession to foreign governments. If anything beneficial came from the rebellion, it was modernization. After 1900, China began a rapid change from traditional industries and customs to those of the more advanced Western nations.

Men of 'C' Troop, 9th US Cavalry at Camp Lawton, Seattle, before embarkation for China. Two other all-Black regiments also served in China: the 24th and 25th Infantry. The white man third from the right is not one of the regiment's officers, but probably a sutler or mule-driver. Note revolvers worn butt-forwards on right hip; Krag-Jorgensen carbine (second from left); and double-banked cartridge loops on Mills belts (left, and second from left). (T. Peiser; Special Collections, Suzzallo Library, University of Washington, Seattle)

For the Allies, the results of the Boxer Rebellion were a little less spectacular. Open hostility to foreigners in China was abolished and the Allies did gain significant concessions, especially in access to natural resources. The strong competition between the Japanese and the Russians was a warning of things to come. Within five years a war would break out between Russia and Japan which would further confirm Japan's dominance in the Far East. The other Allies would become involved in their own 'disagreement' less than fourteen years later with the outbreak of the Great War. Never again would the flags of Austria-Hungary, France, Germany, Great Britain, Italy, Japan, Russia and the United States fly together in an allied military operation against a common enemy.

Chronology

1899

Nov–Dec	Boxer riots against Chinese Christians.
Dec 30	Reverend Brooks murdered by Boxers.

1900

Jan 11	Dowager Empress's decree concerning China's secret societies.
Mid-May	Boxer riots in Pao Ting Fu.
May 27	Foreign ministers ask for Chinese intervention in riots.
May 28	Two British clergymen attacked at Pao Ting Fu.
May 31	Allied troops begin arriving in Peking.
June 4	Last Allied troops arrive in Peking.
June 9	Peking Racecourse destroyed by Boxers. Sir Claude MacDonald requests Admiral Seymour to advance on Peking with reinforcements.
June 10	Telegraph line from Peking cut. Mail service halted. Prince Tuan appointed head of Tsungli Yamen. Seymour column departs Tientsin.
June 11	Chancellor Sugiyama murdered in Peking by Chinese troops. Seymour column reaches Lang Fang.
June 12	Seymour's scouts turned back at An Ting.
June 15	Boxers take Native City of Tientsin. Seymour column forced to retreat.

June 16	Chinese begin mining entrance to Pei Ho. Chinese occupy railroad at Taku.
June 17	Taku Forts bombarded and captured by Allies. Chinese attack International Settlement of Tientsin.
June 19	Tsungli Yamen delivers ultimatum to foreign ministers in Peking demanding all foreigners leave Peking.
June 20	Baron von Ketteler murdered by Chinese troops in Peking. Siege of Legations and Pei T'ang begins.
June 21	China officially declares war on the Allies.
June 22	Admiral Seymour's column captures and entrenches the Hsiku Arsenal.
June 23	International Settlement of Tientsin relieved.
June 26	Seymour column located and rescued by Cossacks.
June 27	Tientsin Arsenal destroyed by Allies.
July 9	Hsiku Arsenal recaptured and destroyed by Allies.
July 14	Native city of Tientsin captured by Allies.
July 17	Cease-fire in Peking—lasts until 25 July.
July 27	Second cease-fire in Peking—lasts until 4 Aug.
Aug 4	Second Allied relief column leaves Tientsin for Peking.
Aug 5	Battle of Pei Tsang.
Aug 6	Battle of Yang Tsun.
Aug 12	Allies occupy Tungchow.
Aug 14	Allies enter Peking and end siege of Legations.
Aug 15	Dowager Empress flees Peking. American assault on Forbidden City.
Aug 16	Siege of Pei T'ang Cathedral ends.
Aug 28	Allied 'victory march' through Forbidden City.
Sep 21	General von Waldersee and German East Asia Brigade arrive at Taku.
Oct 20	Pao Ting Fu captured by the Allies.
Oct 26	Flight of Dowager Empress ends at Sian.
Dec 22	Allied peace proposals presented to Chinese.

1901

Feb 1	Boxer Society abolished.
May 29	China offers to pay £67.5 million indemnity to the Allies.
July 24	Tsungli Yamen abolished.
Sep 7	Peace Protocol of Peking signed by China and the Allies marking the official end to the Boxer Rebellion.

1902

Jan 7	Dowager Empress returns to Peking.

Some of General Tung Fu-hsiang's 'Kansu Braves', who were among the Imperial troops defending Peking. See commentary on colour plate C1. (University of Western Australia Press)

The Armies

The Chinese Army

The Chinese Army can be divided into three major groups. These groups represent primarily the nationalities of the troops:

(i) The Manchu or *Pa chi*. These were the Bannermen, or men of the Eight Bans.
(ii) The regular Chinese troops: the *Lü ying* or Army of the Green Flag; the *Yung* or Brave Ones and the *Lien chün* or New Formations.
(iii) Foreign elements, including Mongols and Tibetan militia.

The Eight Bans were eight divisions of Manchu troops. Each division was organized into four regiments (*Chia-la*) of five companies (*Niu-lu*) comprising roughly 3,000 troops each. Each of the Eight Bans had a colourful flag of its own, and this

1. Private, British Royal Marine Light Infantry
2. Private, US Marine Corps
3. Fusilier-Marin, French Navy
4. Seaman, Russian Navy

A

1. Seaman, Austro-Hungarian Navy
2. Private, Russian Infantry
3. Private, German 3. *Seebataillon*

B

1. Imperial Chinese infantryman, Kansu Braves
2. Boxer
3. Manchu *Ten nai* (Tiger-man)

1. Trooper, Japanese Cavalry
2. Private, Japanese 5th Infantry Regt.
3. Private, H.M. 1st Chinese Regt.

D

1. Private, Italian *Bersaglieri*
2. Private, French Marine Infantry
3. Private, German East Asia Brigade

1. **Imperial Chinese infantryman**
2. **Chinese irregular cavalryman**
3. **Imperial Chinese artilleryman**

1. Sowar, 16th Bengal Lancers
2. Sepoy, 1st Sikhs, Punjab Frontier Force
3. Rifleman, 4th Gurkha Rifles

G

1. Major, Japanese Cavalry
2. Captain, US Infantry
3. Captain, British Royal Welch Fusiliers

H

may be why the troops were referred to as 'Banner-men'. The troops of the Eight Bans were the Emperor's personal army and performed such tasks as providing the Palace Guard of the Imperial Summer Residence (the *Yüan ming yüan*), the Guards of the Imperial Burial Grounds (the *Shou ling ch'in ping*), the Imperial Guard (*Ch'in chün ying*) and the Field Corps (the *Shen chi ying*).

The *Lü ying*, or Army of the Green Flag, were Chinese used as military police for internal security. They were expected to back up the Eight Bans in time of war. The strength of the Army of the Green Flag differed from province to province, but generally followed these organ-zational lines. The overall commander was the General (*T'i tu*) and under him were several brigade commanders (*Tsung ping*). Each brigade (*Chen piao*) was made up of several battalions (*In*). There were four types of battalions; *Ma ping* (infantry, 500 men), *Pu ping* (cavalry, 250 men), *Shou ping* (garrison, various strengths), and *Lien ping* (field troops, various strengths).

The *Yung*, or Brave Ones, were made up of free Chinese who had volunteered for military service. The *Yung* were originally developed to combat internal disorder and threats by the military of the European powers. Many influential Chinese warlords raised units of Brave Ones.

The *Lien chün*, or New Formations, were Chinese troops selected from the best of the Green Flag units. They were not as esteemed as the Manchu Eight Bans, but were considered better than the *Yung* and were better armed.

The Tibetan and Mongolian militia were poorly armed and trained. They were not well organized and were used primarily to protect postal routes in the interior. Some Mongolian horse archers served with the main Chinese Army in the Peking area.

After China's defeat by Japan in 1894–95 the Chinese government allowed several influential Chinese military men to form new army units based on European standards. One of these men, Chang Chih-tung, formed the Self-Strengthening Army (*Tzu-chi'ang chün*), which consisted of thirteen battalions (eight infantry, two cavalry, two artillery and one engineer). Chang hired thirty-five German officers and NCOs to train the army. Each of Chang's units had a distinct organization. Each infantry battalion had five companies of fifty men each, each artillery unit had four batteries of fifty men each, and each cavalry unit had 180 men divided into three squadrons. Late in 1896 Chang organized two new battalions of infantry and another detach-ment of engineers.

A Chinese artillery battery near Peking. (National Army Museum, London)

In late 1895 Yüan Shih-kai reorganized the Pacification Army (*Ting-wu chün*), which had originally been formed in 1894. The infantry was organized into two regiments, one with two battalions, the other with three. The artillery was formed into rapid fire, heavy and reserve batteries. The cavalry was organized into four troops and the engineers into six specialized categories. The total strength of the Pacification Army was listed as 7,000 men.

Two other re-formed armies appeared after the Sino-Japanese War. General Nieh Shih-ch'eng formed the Tenacious Army (*Wu-i chün*) and General Sung Ch'ing formed the Resolute Army (*I-chün*). General Nieh's army had a strength of 10,000 and was based on German organization and training. The troops were superior to most Chinese, but were not as good as Yüan's or Chang's men. By 1898 the Tenacious Army had been equipped with Mauser rifles, Maxim machine guns and various types of modern artillery. Little importance was placed on drill, however, and morale and discipline were poor.

Late in 1898, the Chinese armies in the north were organized into the Guards Army (*Wu wei chün*). Five divisions were organized as follows:

Left Division:	The Resolute Army of Sung Ch'ing
Right Division:	Yüan Shih-K'ai's Army
Front Division:	The Tenacious Army of Shih-ch'eng
Rear Division:	Tung Fu-hsiang's Kansu Braves (described as '10,000 Islamic rabble' by Westerners)
Centre Division:	Newly-formed troops comprised mostly of Bannermen

It was planned that each division would hav eight battalions (*ying*)—five of infantry and on each of cavalry, artillery and engineers. Each battalion would have four companies (*tui*) of 25(men. Only the Right and Centre Divisions appea to have complied with these plans.

After 1860 the Chinese government sought t re-arm its troops with a standardized system o European weapons. Unfortunately, the uniformity failed to materialize and weapons varied from army to army and even from man to man withir each army. In the 1890s some modern Krup

26

field guns as well as some Gatling and Maxim machine guns were acquired. Ammunition was always in short supply, as China had only seven small arsenals to supply an army of over one million men. Target practice and other training which involved the expenditure of ammunition were severely limited or even prohibited.

One weapon which was exclusively Chinese was the *gingal*. By the end of the 19th century most were breech-loaders, though many men still loaded them through the muzzle! The *gingal* had a barrel which was about seven feet long and had a calibre of approximately one inch. The cartridge was smaller in diameter than the bore but contained one large and several small bullets with a large charge of powder. The gun was fired from a prop (somewhat like a Renaissance matchlock) and was best served by a crew of two or three men.

As with weapons, Chinese uniforms were just as confusing and non-standard. Uniforms varied from civilian clothing to very European-looking tunics and breeches. Soldiers of the Eight Bans and the Army of the Green Flag wore a long sleeveless jacket over their civilian clothing. The jacket was usually blue, but red, green and white were also worn. The jacket was trimmed along the front, bottom and arm openings with a contrasting colour—normally yellow, red or white. The jacket had a large cut-out collar and wide stitched fasteners down the front. On the head could be worn a low, flat turban, a silk 'Mandarin' hat with red tassel, or a straw 'coolie' hat.

Troops of the New Formations wore shirts with very full sleeves which were fastened on the side and held in place by a waist sash. Over the shirt was worn a short apron which had two long lobes extending down to the feet on each side. Both the shirt and the apron had colourful borders with woollen designs in the corners. White discs on the front and back of the shirt bore Chinese characters which showed the category, type and unit to which the soldier belonged. Sandals were worn in warm weather. In winter, boots were made from bundled cloth held together by thongs. Headgear could be either the turban, 'Mandarin' hat, or straw 'coolie' hat.

Training and tactics varied as much as the uniforms and weapons of the individual men. Most of the New Formation troops had some European training. The men from the Army of the Green Flag had only minimal training and most of that was based on traditional Chinese weapons and warfare. The Eight Bans also practised classical Chinese warfare and tactics. These troops were formed into eight tactical groups as follows:

(1)	*Ch'ang ch'iang*	Pikemen
(2)	*Ch'ang tao*	Broadswordmen and Halberdiers
(3)	*Niao ch'iang*	Musketeers with short muskets
(4)	*T'ai ch'iang*	Musketeers with long muskets
(5)	*Ta p'ao*	Artillery
(6)	*Ten nai*	Shield bearers, or 'tigers'
(7)	*Kung chiang*	Archers
(8)	*Ma ping*	Cavalry

A typical Eight Ban formation on the battlefield would be a rank of 'tigers' in skirmish order followed by a rank of pikemen followed by a rank of archers. If the unit was armed with muskets, the 'tigers' would be followed by two ranks of musketeers. Cavalry and artillery would support the main formation from the rear or the flanks.

The Allied Armies

To go into depth on the arms, uniforms, equipment, weapons and tactics of all the troops of the eight Allied powers would be beyond the scope of this book. The following is a listing of the actual units which took part in the fighting during the Boxer Rebellion.

Austria-Hungary

The only Austro-Hungarian troops to serve in China were about 400 sailors from the Austrian squadron of warships.

France

The French dispatched the following troops from Indo-China to aid in the relief of Peking. From Saigon came the 1st Battalion, 11th Regiment of Marine Infantry and the 12th Battery, Indo-China Artillery Regiment (six 80mm. mountain guns). From Hanoi came the 1st Battalion, 9th Regiment of Marine Infantry, the 2nd Battalion, 11th Regiment of Marine Infantry; and the 13th Battery, Indo-China Artillery Regiment (six 80mm. mountain guns). There were also Annamite and Tonkinese *tirailleurs*, Algerian *Turcos* and *Chasseurs d'Afrique*. Sailors from the French fleet

An officer and men of H.M. First Chinese Regiment; see also colour plate D3. Note the two sets of slanted bullet-loops on the chest, five each side; and the three lines of 'twist' spaced down the front. (National Army Museum, London)

also played an important rôle in the campaign.

Germany
In China at the start of hostilities were the 3rd *Seebataillon* (1,126 men), one battery of Marine Horse Artillery (111 men), the Kommando Detachment (800 men, some mounted), and sailors from the East Asian Squadron. The East Asia Brigade which was sent to China with Graf von Waldersee consisted of two infantry brigades, each of two regiments, each of two battalions of 812 men each. There was a mounted regiment of Ulans (600 men), a field artillery regiment of three gun and one howitzer batteries, and a pioneer battalion with telegraph and railroad engineer companies. The East Asia Brigade also contained sanitation, train, munitions and other support troops.

Great Britain
One battalion of the Royal Welch Fusiliers, Her Majesty's First Chinese Regiment, and units of Royal Marines and sailors were in the northern part of China at the start of hostilities. An expeditionary corps was quickly formed in India and sent to China. The initial composition of the expeditionary force was:

> *First Infantry Brigade*
>> 7th Bengal Infantry
>> 26th Bombay Infantry
>> 1st Sikh Infantry
>> 24th Punjab Infantry
> *Second Infantry Brigade*
>> 2nd Bengal Infantry
>> 1st Bn. 4th Gurkha Rifles
>> 30th Bombay Infantry
> *Divisional Troops*
>> 12th Battery, Royal Foot Artillery
>> 1st Bengal Lancers
>> 1st Madras Pioneers
>> No. 4 Co., Bengal Sappers and Miners
>> No. 3 Co., Madras Sappers and Miners
>> No. 2 Co., Bombay Sappers and Miners
> *Line of Communication Troops*
>> 22nd Bombay Infantry
>> 3rd Madras Infantry

As the campaign continued, more troops from India entered the fighting. These included the 16th Bengal Lancers, the 3rd Bombay Lancers, the Hyderabad Lancers, the 34th Madras Pioneers, the Hong Kong Artillery, the Hong Kong Regiment, the 6th Burma Battalion, the 6th Jats, the 7th Rajputs, the 24th Bombay Infantry and the 24th and 26th Baluchistan Infantry.

Italy

Italy's contribution to the Allied cause consisted, initially, of sailors from their cruiser squadron in China. A small volunteer contingent was formed in Italy and sent to China after hostilities had begun. A battalion of the famous *Bersaglieri* was formed from one company each from the 1st, 2nd, 4th, 5th, 6th, 8th, 9th and 11th *Bersaglieri* Regiments. In addition to the *Bersaglieri*, the 24th Line Regiment, some volunteers from the *Alpini* and a battery of machine guns were also sent to China. Some engineers accompanied the small expeditionary corps, and a battery of field guns was supplied by the Italian fleet.

Japan

Japan supplied two divisions to the Allied forces in China. Each division had two brigades of infantry, each of two regiments, one regiment of cavalry (three squadrons), a regiment of field artillery containing three battalions each of two four-gun batteries, a battalion of engineers and a commissariat battalion. The infantry regiments were numbered 1st to 24th with the 1st to 4th in the First Division, the 5th to 8th in the Second Division, and so on. The 2nd (*Sendai*) Division was one of the two Japanese divisions to be sent to China.

Russia

Next to Japan, Russia supplied the largest force to the Allied contingent. Most of the Russian troops to serve in the Boxer Rebellion came from her garrisons in Port Arthur and Vladivostok, both of which were in the Amur District. Units from the East Siberian Line, Rifle and Artillery Regiments all took part in the fighting. In the Far East in 1900 were twelve regiments of East Siberian Rifles, twelve battalions of East Siberian Line Infantry, fourteen East Siberian Artillery Batteries, six regiments of Cossacks (Ussuri, Trans-Baikal and Amur), and the Primorski Dragoon Regiment. There were also various fortress, railroad police and other reserve and support troops in the Amur District. Sailors from the Russian Asian fleet also took part in the fighting.

The United States of America

Representing the United States in the war were

Chasseur d'Afrique in China. Light blue jacket with red ecussons or collar patches, red sash, huge red trousers with black leather booting, and white-covered shako. (National Army Museum, London)

29

the 1st, 2nd, 5th, 8th, 9th, 14th, 15th, 24th and 25th Infantry Regiments (9,760 men); the 1st, 3rd, 6th and 9th Cavalry Regiments (3,028 men); the 6th and 7th Artillery Regiments (1,009 men); the 1st Marine Regiment (781 men) and Signal Corps, Engineer, Medical and other support troops (875 men). To this list should be added about 500 Marines and sailors from the ships of the US Far Eastern Squadron.

The Plates

A1: Private, British Royal Marine Light Infantry
The private illustrated here is shown wearing the blue 'work order' tunic, white trousers and blue fatigue cap. The tunic has a narrow braided red shoulder cord, embroidered red bugle horns on both sides of the plain blue collar, and no cuffs. The cap was piped in red around the crown fold. The Royal Marines cap badge is worn on the front left side. The leather equipment was of the Slade-Wallace pattern stained buff or light brown, with brass fittings. The man is armed with the Long Lee-Enfield Rifle.

A2: Private, US Marine Corps
Fifty-six marines and sailors from the battleship *Oregon* and the cruiser *Newark* provided protection for the US Embassy in Peking. Men fought in 'shirt-sleeve' order to combat the heat as much as possible. The khaki campaign hat bears the bronze US Marine Corps badge on the left side of the crown.

Full dress for the US Marines in 1900 consisted of a dark blue tunic with blue collar trimmed in red, red piping down the front and along the bottom seam, and blue cuff slashes trimmed red. The men wore light blue trousers, with an inch-wide red outer seam stripe for NCOs and officers only. White belts replaced the black leather campaign equipment. The campaign hat was set aside and a white helmet was worn as a replacement. The helmet had gilt chin-scales and a gilt spike on top. The bronze eagle-globe-anchor badge was worn on the front of the helmet. In 1900 the US Marines were armed with the Krag-Jorgensen .30 cal. magazine rifle.

Posed photo of two men of the German East Asia Brigade taken in Germany before embarkation. *(Illustrated London News)*

A3: Fusilier-Marin, French Navy
Detachments of sailors from the French cruiser *D'Entrecasteaux* served at both the Legations and the Pei T'ang Cathedral during the siege at Peking. The French sailor's beret could be white or dark blue, with a red pompon and a black ribbon bearing the ship's name in gold letters. At the ends of the 'tails' of the ribbon were gold anchors. The men could wear either a white or a dark blue blouse with light blue seaman's collar trimmed with three white stripes. The trousers, likewise, could be either white or dark blue. Any combination of white or blue beret, blouse and trousers could have been worn at any one time.

For shore duty, canvas leggings were usually worn. In tropical service a straw hat similar to the British sennet hat was also worn. Belts and equipment were of black leather. The rifle was the same as that carried by the French infantry, the Lebel.

A4: Seaman, Russian Navy
Russian sailors dressed in very similar fashion to the seamen of other nations. The normal uniform consisted of a blue seaman's cap with a very long ribbon bearing the ship's name in gold letters. The blouse and trousers could be either dark blue or white. The collar on the blouse was light blue with white stripe trim.

The intense mid-summer heat of Peking forced many men to remove their blouses and fight wearing just their red-striped shirts, trousers and light equipment. This man is armed with the Russian 'three-line' rifle of .299 cal. (a Russian 'line' being just under one-tenth of an inch). He is wearing as equipment only a small black leather cartridge box over his shoulder.

B1: Seaman, Austro-Hungarian Navy
As with many of the other sailors who fought for the other Allied powers, this man is dressed in the more or less 'standard' naval kit of the period. The white uniform can be considered as 'tropical' or 'summer service' issue. On the right shoulder was worn a special piece of black leather to protect the seaman's blouse from the oil of his Mannlicher rifle. Sailors from the cruiser *Zenta* were Austria-Hungary's prime representatives during the fighting of the Boxer Rebellion.

B2: Private, Russian Infantry
The Russian infantryman pictured here is typical of most of the Russian soldiers who fought with the Allies. The heavy green winter tunic has given way to the summer service *kittel*, an almost shape-less sack coat which was gathered under the waist-belt and then allowed to flare out below. Unit distinction was marked by the shoulder straps—yellow for line infantry; raspberry red for rifles; bright red for artillery; and brown for engineers. The trousers were made of dark green (almost black) cloth. The peakless cap was white in summer and dark green in winter. It is not clear whether the summer cap was merely the

winter cap worn with a white cover. In addition to the change in colour the winter cap also had the unit's branch colour in a wide band around the base. The man is armed with the Russian 'three-line' rifle.

B3: Private, German Third Seebataillon
The German Navy maintained three battalions of marines to protect its foreign naval bases. During the Boxer Rebellion, the 3rd *Seebataillon* left its station at Tsingtao and fought with the Allies against the Chinese. Full dress uniform for these troops consisted of a medium blue jacket and trousers. The jacket had white Swedish cuffs and white shoulder-straps. The collar and cuff slashes were yellow. The trouser seam stripes were also white. A *Jäger* shako bore a gilt eagle badge and black-white-red national cockade.

A more comfortable and practical khaki uniform was worn in summer. This uniform lacked all distinctions except for white shoulder-straps. On the straps in yellow were the Imperial crown over crossed anchors above the Roman numeral of the unit—in this case 'III'. The shako was replaced with a white cork helmet with a white metal badge consisting of a crowned Imperial eagle on an anchor. Below the badge was a small national cockade. A khaki cover for the helmet was issued but not always worn. Arms consisted of a 7.92mm. M98 rifle and bayonet.

C1: Infantryman, Kansu Braves
The Rear Division of the Chinese Guards Army (*Wu wei chün*) provided the majority of the Imperial troops in and around Peking during the Boxer Rebellion. Most of the Rear Division was made up from units of the *Yung*, or Brave Ones, from Kansu Province in western China. As they were recently raised from units of the Brave Ones, many of these soldiers had not yet been issued with the 'standard' Imperial uniform of blue jacket trimmed with yellow lace and black silk 'Mandarin' hat. Instead, the men still wore their *Yung* uniforms.

The low turban was made of dark red cloth with a pattern printed on it in darker red and black. The jacket is primarily red with a wide band of yellow down the right front and around the collar. Separating the red from the yellow is blue trim and piping. The black Chinese characters appearing on the man's chest identify him as being from the 'centre section of the bodyguard of the officer commanding the army' (in other words, General Tung Fu-hsiang's personal guard). The jacket has full, loose sleeves and extends well below the waist-belt. Under the jacket is worn a sort of apron which has two long lobes extending down the sides of the legs. These lobes are yellow with a red panel inserted and trimmed with blue lace. In the centre of the red panel is a white disc bearing the Chinese character *Yung* (Brave), which identifies this man as being from a unit of the Brave Ones.

This particular soldier is carrying a Martini-Henry rifle with socket bayonet. His cartridge-belt is of the woven webbed pattern, similar to the US Mills belts. He carries a large supply of ammunition as it is quite possible that when he runs out of cartridges, he will discard his rifle and pick up another one from a dead enemy or comrade.

C2: Boxer

As all of the Boxers were civilians, they wore no real uniform; the closest thing to a uniform was a piece of red cloth somewhere on their person. This piece of red cloth could be a turban, apron or waist sash. Some men embroidered Chinese characters on the fronts of their jackets. Many, like this man, chose to wear the character *Yung* (Brave). If the turban was not worn, a straw 'coolie' hat would have been the usual replacement. The Boxers could be barefoot or could wear slippers or sandals.

Boxers disliked Western weapons. Their movement preached the overthrow of 'foreign devils' through the use of the martial arts and traditional Chinese weapons. Most Boxers preferred to carry swords, spears and halberds. The swords were wide-bladed chopping weapons, some requiring two-handed use. The spears had long curved blades, while the halberds were of purely Chinese design and did not resemble the halberds of medieval Europe. Some men carried wicker or brass shields.

C3: Manchu Ten nai (Tiger-man)

The *Ten nai*, or Tiger-men, were an integral part of most of the formations of the *Pa chi*, or Manchu Bannermen. The *Ten nai* were used as skirmishers in the Manchu battle formations. Armed with a long sabre and a grappling hook on a chain, they were intended to break up cavalry charges.

The Tiger-man wears a sleeveless jacket with wide stripes alternating yellow-orange and black apparently imitating tigerskin. The shirt and pants are of light blue cloth. This man wears a yellow cloth turban, but a straw 'coolie' hat could also be worn. The side aprons, similar to those worn by the Brave Ones, were dark blue with yellow trim around the edge.

The bright uniform of the *Ten nai*, combined with loud yelling, was intended to scare away enemy cavalry. If these tactics did not work, the Tiger-men were supposed to break up the enemy cavalry charges with their sabres and grappling hooks. The painted shield which this man carries bears a brightly painted face with the Chinese character *Wang* (king) above the face's forehead. 'King' is a lesser title which has probably been presented to the commander of this particular unit of the *Ten nai* by the Emperor.

D1: Trooper, Japanese Cavalry

The Japanese army was dressed in very practical uniforms based on those of the French and German armies. The uniform of the Japanese cavalry trooper in 1900 was a dark blue dolman with red frogging across the chest and fifteen brass buttons. At the end of each row of frogging was a brass button and a double loop of frogging which hung from the button. The collar was dark blue with red trim and the shoulder-straps were plain blue. On the back of the dolman was hussar-style seam lacing extending from the bottom of the dolman and ending behind the shoulder blade in a trefoil. There was also red trim down the front of the dolman and along the bottom edge.

The peaked cap was dark blue with red piping and a red band. On the front of the red band was a brass star. The trousers were dark blue with a red seam stripe, tucked into black knee-high boots. This man is armed with the Meiji 30th year carbine (which was based on the German Mauser design) slung over the left shoulder by means of a conventional shoulder-strap rather

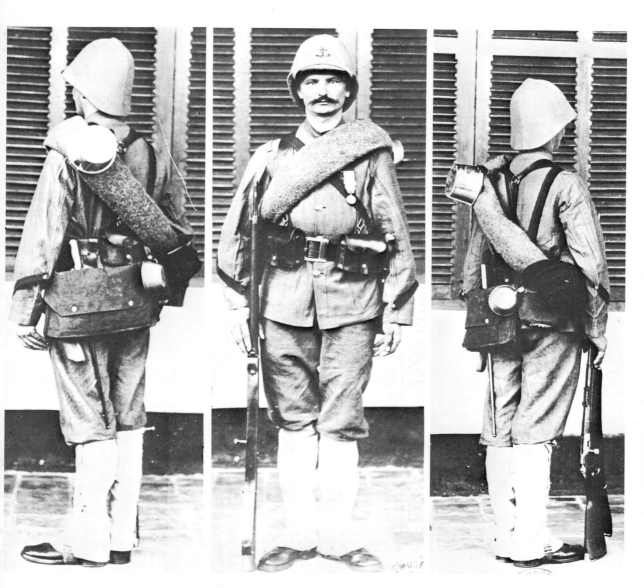

Three angles on a French Marine infantryman in the blue uniform worn in China; see also colour plate E2. Behind the right hip the ends of the blanket roll are thrust into the képi, which hangs by its chinstrap from the belt. It is dark blue with red piping and, instead of the regulation anchor, a red '9'. (Musée de l'Armée)

than a carbine sling. The trooper carries a simple, slightly curved sabre with a red sword knot, in a plain polished steel scabbard.

In summer, a light khaki or white linen uniform replaced the dark blue. A khaki or white cover with neck cloth was worn over the cap. The summer service uniform had no branch or rank distinctions except for the coloured cap band.

D2: Private, Japanese Infantry

The Japanese infantry also wore a predominantly blue uniform during the Boxer Rebellion. The tunic had a red standing collar piped dark blue around the top. The shoulder-straps were red, with the regimental number in blue. The cap was dark blue with yellow piping and a wide yellow band. A brass star ornamented the centre front of the yellow band.

Regulations included dark blue trousers with a red outer seam stripe, but on campaign the men usually wore white linen summer service trousers. A light-weight uniform in white or khaki was worn in warmer weather. The cap had a neckcloth similar to that worn by the cavalry. Leggings were khaki and the shoes were rough leather with hobnailed soles. When the full pack was not worn, a blanket roll was worn over the left shoulder. This man is armed with the Meiji 30th Year rifle with bayonet.

D3: Private, Her Majesty's 1st Chinese Regiment
When the Royal Navy established its base at Wei-Hai-Wei, a regiment of Chinese was raised to act as the local constabulary. The unit was commanded by British officers and, in 1900, had seven companies numbering 420 men. During the Boxer Rebellion the 1st Chinese Regiment was present at all of the major actions except Pao Ting Fu.

The men wore a curious combination of local clothing with cast-off Royal Navy and British Army equipment. The loose-fitting tunic and trousers were made of khaki cloth. Around the waist was a red or white sash (accounts and photographs do not agree on the colour; perhaps both were worn, possibly by different companies). On the breast of the tunic were sewn two sets of cartridge loops. Belts were brown leather Royal Navy pattern, as were the cartridge pouches. Shoes were black and the puttees were dark blue. The straw hat was of the Royal Navy sennet pattern with a plain khaki pagri. A khaki cover was issued for the hat, but was not always worn. The men were not allowed to wear the traditional Chinese pigtail. Arms consisted of a Martini-Henry rifle with socket bayonet.

E1: Private, Italian Bersaglieri
When the *Bersaglieri* left Italy for China in the summer of 1900, they took with them their dress blue uniform and a khaki field service uniform. The khaki uniforms did not stand up well to the campaigning and, by the winter of 1900–01, most of the men were wearing their warmer blue uniforms. The light khaki uniform was simple and lacked decorations and insignia except for white metal stars on the front corners of the collar. The white tropical service helmet had a khaki cover, but it was not always worn. A bunch of black-green cock feathers, the symbol of the *Bersaglieri*, was worn through a hole in the khaki cover.

The collar of the blue uniform was black with white metal stars in the crimson 'flames'. The shoulder-straps were dark blue with crimson piping. The blue trousers had crimson piping

Three *Bersaglieri*, in the short-lived khaki summer uniform and helmet covers. (National Army Museum, London)

down the outside seams. Regulations called for white canvas gaiters, but in China it appears that the men wore just their ankle-high black boots. The white helmet had a large national cockade in red-white-green with the brass helmet plate superimposed. The badge consisted of crossed rifles, bugle and flaming grenade with a cut-out number '5' on the grenade. All leather equipment was black. The men were armed with the 1891 6.5mm. Parravicino-Carcano rifle and bayonet.

E2: Private 1st Class, French Marine Infantry
Three battalions from the 9th and 11th Marine Infantry fought in China during the Boxer Rebellion. The summer uniform worn by the men in China consisted of a white tropical helmet with a blue cover, a blue single-breasted tunic and blue trousers. The blue material was a denim cloth of faded 'mechanic's blue'. The tunic was fastened down the front by five copper buttons. The gaiters were of heavy white canvas. The helmet badge was a copper 'foul anchor'. Some men wore white linen trousers. Winter gear worn in China consisted of a large beret ornamented with a red anchor, a wool overcoat and a sleeveless sheepskin jacket worn with the fleece inward. Belts and equipment were of black leather. When the full pack was not worn, a grey blanket roll

was worn over the left shoulder. This man wears the Lebel rifle equipment.

E3: Private, German East Asia Brigade

The East Asia Brigade was formed and outfitted quickly in Germany during the summer of 1900. The uniforms were officially field grey, but differences in materials, dye batches and suppliers created a wide variety in the shades worn by the troops. In general, the jacket (*litewka*) was of a slightly darker shade than the hat or trousers. Only in the cavalry does the colour of the tunic appear to be lighter than the trousers.

The hat was made of grey felt and trimmed along the edge of the brim with poppy red (light green for *Jägers*). The hat band was in the branch colour (white for infantry; light green for *Jägers*; poppy red for cavalry; black with poppy red trim for artillery, pioneers and railroad troops), but photographs indicate that this was not worn in China. The hat was turned up on the right side and a black-white-red national cockade was attached to the upper edge of the turned-up brim. Beneath the national cockade was worn a small cockade from the soldier's home province, in this case the blue-white-blue of Bavaria.

The model 1892 *litewka* is of field grey cloth and is fastened down the front by six horn buttons. There are four large pockets on the front of the jacket and, unusually, two in the rear. The two lower front pockets were intended to carry cartridges, and were lined with leather to improve wear. The collar, front seam of the jacket and pocket flaps were trimmed in poppy red for all branches except *Jägers*, who had light green trim. The shoulder-straps were reversible for either field or garrison duty. When in the field, the straps were field grey trimmed with poppy red (light green for *Jägers*). For garrison duty, the shoulder-straps were of a solid colour in the unit's branch colour—white for infantry, light green for *Jägers*, poppy red for cavalry, artillery, pioneer and railroad troops. The shoulder-straps of the infantry bore the unit's number embroidered in red. Artillery had a red grenade, pioneers a red 'P' and railroad troops a red 'E' and lightning bolt.

Boots were of red-brown leather. All other belts and pouches were of 'greenish-brown' leather. A bread sack was worn on the left hip and a canteen

A **Russian Cossack in China, 1900. (National Army Museum, London)**

on the right hip. The rifle was the Model 1898 Mauser, which fired a five-round clip. Each of the cartridge pouches carried three clips for the rifle.

For summer service a light-weight khaki uniform and tropical helmet with khaki cover were issued. The cut and style of this uniform was very similar to that of the German *Seebataillon* (see Plate B3). Shoulder-strap colours for garrison and field duty remained the same for the khaki uniform. The *Jägers* adopted a strange flat-topped sun helmet for their tropical kit, apparently attempting to pattern it after their shako.

F1: Chinese infantryman in 'Westernized' uniform

When China allowed several of its more influential

military leaders to raise new armies in the late 1890s, several of them adopted European arms, equipment and uniforms. The man shown here is wearing a 'Westernized' uniform consisting of a pull-over blouse, trousers and peakless cap in blue cloth. On the front of the tunic was a white patch of cloth which bore Chinese characters identifying the man's rank and the unit to which he belonged. The shoulder-straps were of plain yellow cloth with no insignia; the left strap concealed the fastening of the blouse, which buttoned along the top of the shoulder. Leather belts and equipment were black. The rifle is a Model 1888 Austrian 8mm Mannlicher.

None of the contemporary illustrations on which this figure is based identify the exact unit which he represents. It is most likely that he is from either Chang Chih-tung's Self-Strengthening Army (*Tzu-ch'iang chün*) or from Yüan Shih-kai's Pacification Army (*Ting-wu chün*). Both of these men stressed Western equipment and training when they formed their new military units. Note the one remaining link to China's old military—the man's pigtail extending down his back from under his cap!

F2: Chinese irregular cavalryman

China's greatest weakness in its wars of the late 19th century was a lack of effective cavalry. The few well-trained and equipped cavalry in the regular Chinese units were with Yüan Shih-kai (who was fighting with the Allies), and with Chang Chih-tung (who was not involved in the fighting). China depended primarily on irregular cavalry from Mongolia and western China to perform scouting and communications duties.

The cavalryman pictured here is typical of these irregulars. The hat is of animal skin with the fur side turned in. The overcoat and other clothing are of typical civilian cut and colour. The only things identifying this man as a soldier are his arms, which include a Mauser carbine, bow and arrows, curved sword and whip. The bow is carried in a combination bow-case and quiver, the style of which dates back to ancient times. The most interesting items of his equipment are the stirrups, which are made from a bent piece of metal, very different from those used by Western cavalry. This man is mounted on a small, shaggy

Asiatic pony much like those ridden by Genghis Khan and his followers centuries before.

F3: Chinese artilleryman

This particular uniform is that worn by Li Hung-chang's artillery during the late 1890s, but it could be considered typical of those worn by all Chinese artillerymen. This man wears a green turban, a yellow vest with a red design on the chest and wide red stripes top and bottom, and very full light blue trousers which reached to just below the knee. The shirt worn under the vest was blue with red cuffs. The lower legs were covered by black stockings, and white slipper-type shoes were worn. Belts and equipment were of brown leather.

Other Chinese artillery units wore uniforms in similar styles but with darker primary colours—predominantly blues and reds. The cut and style of the uniforms were similar and followed the typical Chinese pattern. Units were armed with a variety of cannon and rapid fire weapons, dating from 18th century muzzle-loaders to modern Krupp, Maxim and Gatling guns. Chinese artillerymen were probably the best trained of all the Chinese Imperial troops. In several of the actions fought with the Allies the Chinese gunfire silenced the Allied guns or forced them to limber-up and move off.

G1: Sowar, 16th Bengal Lancers

By 1900 even the colourful *pagris* of the Indian Cavalry Regiments had vanished except for full dress occasions. This trooper of the 16th Bengal Lancers is wearing a plain khaki *pagri* (turban), khaki *kurta* and puttees. Shoulder-scales on the *kurta* were of polished steel links.

G2: Sepoy, 1st Sikh Infantry (Punjab Frontier Force)

This regiment, raised in 1846, was senior among the infantry regiments of the Punjab Frontier Force, that part of the Indian Army which had a special responsibility for keeping the peace on the North-West Frontier. It was one of the first Indian regiments to leave for China in 1900 and, with the 7th Rajputs, was the first of the British contingent to enter the besieged Legations at Peking.

This sepoy has a yellow fringe of the regimental

facing colour to his khaki *pagri*. The Indian soldier's service dress consisted of a khaki drill *kurta* with loose trousers and puttees. His equipment is the Indian version of the contemporary British Slade-Wallace pattern made of brown leather; in addition to the two pouches worn on the front of the belt, a third of the same pattern as the Gurkha rifleman's (see Plate G3) was worn at the back of the belt. A haversack and water-bottle of Indian pattern were also carried. His firearm is the .303in. Lee-Metford magazine rifle with $12\frac{1}{4}$in. bladed bayonet.

G3: Rifleman, 4th Gurkha Rifles

The 4th Gurkha Rifles, raised in 1857, was the only regiment of Gurkhas to serve in the Boxer Rebellion. The rifleman wears a Kilmarnock cap with a khaki cover, to which a peak and curtain were sometimes fitted when in the field. His *kurta*, which has black buttons as befitting a Rifle regiment, is similar to the sepoy's in Plate G2 but shorter in the skirt. Gurkhas wore narrower trousers, more like those of the British infantry instead of the 'pyjama' type of the rest of the Indian infantry. His accoutrements are of black

leather and have larger, more flexible pouches than the brown leather type of the regular Indian units. The *kukri* carried by all Gurkhas is suspended from the waist-belt behind his right hip. His rifle is the same as that carried by the Sikh in Plate G2.

H1: Major, Japanese Cavalry

Japanese officers tended to wear the same cut, style and colour uniforms as their men with a few 'personal' touches added. On the cap, a brass button stamped with the Imperial emblem, a chrysanthemum, replaces the star worn by the rank and file. The colour of the frogging on the dolman has changed from red to black, but otherwise remains the same. Black lace trim in the form of a 'crow's foot' adorns each cuff of the dolman. The slightly curved sabre is carried in a plain polished steel scabbard suspended from the waist-belt by means of black leather belts worn under the dolman. A black leather waist-belt with pistol holster and a small cartridge pouch would

37

Group of Japanese infantry and cavalry, officers and other ranks, wearing both blue winter and white summer uniforms. (National Army Museum, London)

also normally be worn. Boots were of polished black leather.

H2: Captain, US Infantry
By 1900 the US Army had adopted a very neat and practical khaki tropical service uniform. The khaki campaign hat was worn with gold cords by all officers. The plain collar of the khaki tunic is decorated with the national coat of arms and the crossed rifles of the infantry. On the light blue shoulder-straps are worn the twin silver bars signifying the rank of captain. The light blue shoulder-straps worn by the officer in this plate were the final remnant of the branch-of-service colour distinctions to go into the field.

The khaki breeches laced up to the knees and were usually covered below the knees by brown leather leggings which fastened by means of straps. Equipment included a waist-belt with brass buckle bearing the national coat of arms, a brown leather pistol holster, with sometimes a cartridge box or bullet loops on the belt and a canteen. Weapons were a .38 or .45 cal. revolver and a short infantry sword in a polished steel scabbard.

H3: Officer, Royal Welch Fusiliers
The 2nd Battalion, Royal Welch Fusiliers was the only regular unit of the British Army to serve in the Boxer Rebellion. The officer pictured here wears the khaki Foreign Service tunic, breeches and helmet with khaki pagri. The scarlet badge worn on the helmet has a flaming grenade in white with the words 'Royal Welch Fusiliers' extending around it. The equipment is of the well-known 'Sam Browne' pattern. The 1897 pattern infantry sword is carried in a brown leather scabbard. A revolver, usually of .38 cal., completed the officer's kit.

Notes sur les planches en couleur

A1 Notez le bord supérieur du calot, qui est gansé de rouge; insigne de la Royal Marine représentant un globe et des feuilles de laurier, porté à gauche et à l'avant du calot; des insignes représentant un cor de chasse sont portés sur le col. Courroies et bourses du type Slade-Wallace; fusil 'long' Lee-Enfield. **A2** Insigne de l'U.S.M.C. représentant un globe, un aigle et une ancre, porté sur le côté gauche du chapeau de brousse; notez l'équipement en cuir qui est encore porté par ces troupes, malgré la distribution répandue à l'armée de équipement Mills en toile à sangles. Fusil Kraf-Jorgensen. **A3** Tenue tropicale; équipement pour fusil Lebel. **A4** Vêtu seulement d'un maillot rayé et d'un pantalon à bas évasés, ce marin ne porte qu'une cartouchière sur une courroie croisée; l'arme est le fusil russe à trois lignes'.

B1 Des marins du navire 'Zenta' étaient la contribution principale de l'Autriche-Hongrie à la force internationale. Fusil Männlicher; notez le coussinet en cuir sur l'épaulette en droite, dont le but était de protéger la blouse blanche contre les tâches d'huile émanant du fusil. **B2** Le kittel blanc et la housse blanche qui couvrait la casquette étaient portés en été par l'infanterie russe: épaulette jaune pour l'infanterie de ligne. **B3** Ce bataillon était normalement en garnison à Tsingtao. Tenue d'été kaki épaulettes blanches avec l'insigne d'une couronne, des ancres croisées et le chiffre romain 'III'. Fusil M1898 et équipement. Une housse kaki était quelquefois portée sur le casque.

C1 Les troupes impériales chinoises à Pékin appartenaient pour la plupart aux arrières de l'Armée des Gardes (*Wu wei chun*) formée à partir d'unités recrutées des 'Yung' ou 'Courageux' dans la province du Kansu. Ce soldat porte encore les vêtements d'un Yung et est armé d'un fusil Martini-Henry. **C2** Les Boxers portaient une tenue civile avec l'addition d'un article de couleur rouge—un turban, une ceinture, etc... Le caractère représentant le mot 'Yung'—'Courageux'—est porté sur la poitrine. Les armes occidentales étaient méprisées en faveur des armes traditionnelles chinoises. **C3** 'Les Hommes-tigres' (*Ten nai*) étaient des tirailleurs dans l'armée mandchoue qui utilisaient leurs chaînes à grappins ainsi que leurs sabres pour rompre les attaques de la cavalerie ennemie.

D1 Uniforme simple, inspiré du style occidental, porté par les soldats de la cavalerie japonaise à cette époque; un dolman bleu foncé à galon rouge et une casquette bleue à bande rouge identifiaient la cavalerie. **D2** Les soldats d'infanterie semblent avoir porté leur tunique bleue d'hiver avec le pantalon blanc de la tenue d'été. La bande et la ganse jaunes sur la casquette identifient l'infanterie; comme celui de la cavalerie, l'insigne de la casquette est une étoile en laiton. Le numéro du régiment est marqué sur les épaulettes. Fusil Meiji dit '30 ans'. **D3** Unité locale de police recrutée par la Royal Navy pour policer la région de leur base à Wei-hai-wei; au nombre d'environ 420, avec des officiers britanniques, le régiment s'est battu dans la plupart des principaux engagements de la guerre. Uniforme ample en kaki, chapeau ennet' de la Royal Navy et équipement Royal Navy en cuir; fusil Martini-Henry.

E1 L'uniforme tropical en kaki avait été emmené en Chine mais il s'est avéré inadéquat et la grande tenue bleue était donc portée en campagne. Notez

Farbtafeln

A1 Zu bemerken ist der rote Schnurbesatz am oberen Rand der Feldmütze; links vorne auf der Mütze befindet sich das Royal Marine Emblem von Erdkugel mit Lorbeerkranz; Jagdhorn Insignien auf dem Kragen. Slade-Wallace Gurt mit Patronentaschenausrüstung; 'Langes' Lee-Enfield-Gewehr. **A2** U.S.M.C. Erdkugel, Adler und Anker-Emblem auf der linken Seite des Schlapphuts; bemerkenswert ist es, dass diese Truppen immer noch lederne Gurtausrüstung tragen, trotz der allgemeinen Heeresausgabe von der aus Gewebe hergestellten Mills-Ausrüstung. Krag-Jorgensen Gewehr. **A3** Tropische Uniform; Lebel Gewehrausrüstung. **A4** Bis auf das gestreifte Hemd und die unten weiten Hosen ausgezogen, trägt dieser Matrose nur eine Patronentasche auf Quergurt; die Waffe ist das russische 'Drei-Linien' Gewehr.

B1 Matrosen aus der 'Zenta' bildeten den oesterreichischen Hauptbeitrag zu den internationalen Streitkräften. Mannlichergewehr, bemerkenswert ist die lederne Unterlage am rechten Schulter, um Gewehröl von der weissen Bluse fernzuhalten. **B2** Weisser Kittel und Mützenüberzug von der russischen Infanterie im Sommer getragen; durch das gelbe Schulterbrett wird Linieninfanterie erkannt. 'Drei-Linien' Gewehr. **B3** Dieses Bataillon war normalerweise in Tsingtao stationiert. Khaki Sommeruniform mit weissen Schulterbrettern worauf eine Krone, gekreuzte Anker und römische Nummer III aufgetragen sind. M1898 Gewehr und Ausrüstung. Einen khaki Helmüberzug wurde auch manchmal getragen.

C1 Die kaiserlichen chinesischen Truppen in Peking waren hauptsächlich von der rückwärtigen Division des Gardeheeres (*Wu wei chun*), und bestand aus Einheiten, die im Kansuprovinz von den 'Yung' oder 'Tapferen' ausgehoben wurden. Dieser Soldat trägt immer noch seine Yung Bekleidung und ist mit einem Martini-Henry Gewehr bewaffnet. **C2** Boxer Aufständige trugen Zivilkleider, gewöhnlicherweise mit Zusatz eines roten Gegenstandes—Turban, Leibbinde, usw. Das Schriftzeichen Yung, 'tapfer', wird auf der Brust getragen. Westliche Waffen wurden zugunsten traditioneller chinesischer Waffen verachtet. **C3** Die 'Tigermänner' (*ten nai*) waren leichtbewaffnete Plänkler im Manchuheere, die ihre auf Ketten befestigte Enterhaken und Säbel gebraucht haben, feindliche Kavallerieangriffe zu erschüttern und auseinanderzutreiben.

D1 Einfache von den westlichen Mächten beeinflusste Uniform der japanischen Kavallerie der Periode: dunkelblauer Dolman mit rotem Schnurbesatzverzierung und eine blaue Schirmmütze mit rotem Kavallerieidentifizierendem Band. **D2** Scheinbar haben die Infanteristen den blauen Winterwaffenrock zusammen mit den weissen Hosen der Sommeruniform getragen. Infanterie wird durch den gelben Band und Schnurbesatz der Mütze gekennzeichnet; wie bei der Kavallerie, besteht das Einheitsemblem auf der Mütze aus einem Stern. Regimentsnummer wird auf die Achselklappen angebracht: Meiji '30 Jahr' Gewehr. **D3** Einheimische Gendarmerie von der Royal Navy

Russian infantrymen in white summer service *kittel* and cap; note ranking on yellow shoulder-boards of two NCOs at left. (National Army Museum, London)

l'absence de guêtres. **E2** Trois bataillons de marsouins avaient été amenés d'Indo-Chine pour la campagne des Boxers, habillés en uniforme de toile 'bleu de mécanicien'. Equipement pour fusil Lebel. Notez le brassard boutonné sur l'avant-bras portant la rayure du rang. **E3** Les photos montrent que le chapeau et le pantalon sont d'un gris plus pâle que celui de la tunique. La ganse rouge indique l'infanterie de ligne. Notez la cocarde inférieure sur le chapeau, aux couleurs de l'état bavarois, et la différence de teinte entre les bottes et les bourses.

F1 La blouse se fermait avec des boutons cachés sous l'épaulette gauche. Le rang et l'unité sont identifiés par les caractères imprimés sur le morceau de tissu blanc appliqué sur la poitrine. Notez la queue. **F2** Les forces impériales avaient de bons cavaliers et comptaient pour la plupart sur des irréguliers de Mongolie et des steppes occidentales. **F3** Les artilleurs étaient probablement les mieux formés de tous les soldats impériaux; ils avaient un mélange de mitrailleuses Krupp, Maxim et Gatling, ainsi que de vieux canons se chargeant par la bouche.

G1 Tenue typique de la cavalerie indienne à cette époque, ne variant que peu d'une unité à une autre. **G2** Un régiment de vétérans du garnison de la frontière du nord-ouest indien, les 1ers Sikhs étaient parmi les premières troupes à pénétrer dans les légations assiégées à Pékin à la tête de la force de secours. **G3** Les boutons noirs, les insignes et l'équipement habituels des régiments de fusiliers. Le célèbre couteau appelé le kukri était suspendu sur la hanche droite.

H1 Un uniforme simple de style occidental, orné de galon noir; un bouton gravé du motif d'un chrysanthème remplace l'insigne d'une étoile porté par les troupes sur la casquette. **H2** Galon d'or de chapeau; les armoiries nationales ainsi que l'insigne de l'infanterie paraissent des deux côtés du col; notez également les épaulettes bleues, le dernier vestige des couleurs distinctives portées sur la tenue de campagne et représentant les différentes branches de service. **H3** Le 2ème Bataillon des Royal Welch Fusiliers était le seul bataillon de l'infanterie britannique à se battre dans cette campagne. L'insigne du casque est une grenade blanche avec le titre du régiment en haut et en bas, sur fond rouge.

French sailors kitted out for infantry fighting *(fusiliers-marins)* **boarding a train in Tientsin. They wear white summer uniforms with straw hats very similar to the British 'sennet' type; Lebel rifle equipment; blue-grey haversacks; and old rectangular water canteens, very like British canteens of the two World Wars, covered in blue-grey cloth. (Major A. McK. Annand)**

angewerbt ihren Flottenstützpunkt zu Wei-hai-wei polizeilich zu überwachen: 420 Mann stark mit britischen Offizieren, hat das Regiment an allen bedeutenden Einsätzen des Krieges teilgenommen. Lose Khakiuniform mit Royal Navy *'sennet'*-Hut, Royal Navy lederne Ausrüstung; Martini-Henry Gewehr.

E1 Die khaki tropische Uniform ist nach China mitgenommen worden, hat sich aber bald für ungeeignet erwiesen; deswegen wurde die blaue Parade-uniform im Felde getragen. Die Abwesenheit von Gamaschen ist bemerkenswert. **E2** Drei Bataillone von 'marsouin' wurden von Hinterindien für den Boxerfeldzug versetzt und wurden in 'schlosserblauer' Drillichuniform gekleidet. Lebel Gewehrausrüstung. Zu bemerken ist das angeknöpfte Rangabzeichen am Arm. **E3** In Fotos sieht man, dass der Hut und die Hosen eines helleren Graus sind als der Waffenrock. Roter Schnurbesatz kennzeichnet Linieninfanterie. Bemerkenswert ist die untere Hutkokarde in staatlichen bayerischen Farben und der Farbtonunterschied zwischen Stiefel und Patronentaschen.

F1 Bluse mit unter der linken Achselklappe versteckter Knopfbefestigung. Rang und Einheit werden durch die Schriftzeichen auf dem weissen Tuchaufsatz auf der Brust gekennzeichnet. Zu bemerken ist der Zopf. **F2** Die kaiserlichen Streitkräfte waren schwach an guter Kavallerie und müssten sich auf irreguläre Reiter aus Mongolien und den westlichen Steppen verlassen. **F3** Unter den kaiserlichen Truppen ist wahrscheinlich die Artillerie am besten ausgeübt gewesen; sie ist mit einem Gemisch von Krupp-, Maxim- und Gatling-geschütze sowohl als mit Vorderlader aus alter Zeit bewaffnet gewesen.

G1 Typische Felduniform der indischen Kavallerie dieser Periode; die Einheiten liessen sich nur durch Kleinigkeiten unterscheiden. **G2** Ein kampferprobtes Regiment der Garnison der indischen Nordwestgrenze, sind die 1. Sikhs unter den ersten Truppen gewesen, die an der Spitze der Entsatztruppen in die pekinger Legationen eingetreten sind. Zu bemerken ist die gelbe Franse am Turban. Slade-Wallace Ausrüstung indischen Musters und Lee-Metford Gewehr. **G3** Schwarze Knöpfe, Embleme und Ausrüstung, wie bei 'Rifle'-Regimenten üblich war. Das bekannte Kukri-Messer hing hinter der rechten Hüfte.

H1 Eine einfache Uniform westliches Musters mit Schnurbesatz aus schwarzer Litze; der Stern des Mützenemblems der gemeinen Soldaten wird durch einen Knopf mit Chrysanthemmuster ersetzt. **H2** Goldkorde am Hut; auf jeder Kragenspitze sind sowohl das Nationalemblem als das Infanteriekennzeichen angebracht. Bemerkenswert sind die blauen Achselklappen, an letzte Überbleibsel der unterschiedlichen Waffenfarben der verschiedenen Heeresgattungen, das auf der Felduniform noch zu sehen war. **H3** Das zweite Bataillon der Royal Welch Fusiliers war das einzige aktive Infanteriebataillon das in diesem Feldzuge teilgenommen hat. Das Helmemblem besteht aus einer weissen Granate auf einem roten Tuchflicken mit Regimentsname oben und unten.